Reasons To Believe

Evidence for the Christian Message

Chris Schansberg

Alertness Books
▽▲▽

Copyright © 2004 by Christopher R. Schansberg

All rights reserved. No part of this publication may be reproduced, stored in a retrieval system, or transmitted in any form by any means, electronic, mechanical, photocopy, recording or otherwise, without the permission of the author, except as provided by USA copyright law.

Unless otherwise noted, all Scripture quotations have been taken from HOLY BIBLE, NEW INTERNATIONAL VERSION®. Copyright © 1973, 1978, 1984 by International Bible Society. Used by permission of Zondervan Publishing House.

Scripture quotations marked (NLT) are taken from the Holy Bible, New Living Translation, copyright 1996. Used by permission of Tyndale House Publishers, Inc., Wheaton, Illinois 60189. All rights reserved.

Published by:
Alertness Books
P.O. Box 25686
Greenville, SC 29616
Phone: 1-864-444-3728

Fax: 1-413-622-9441
Email:
altertness@policyofliberty.net

Distributed by:

(USA)
Lightning Source Inc.
1246 Heil Quaker Blvd.
La Vergne, TN USA 37086
Voice: (615) 213-5815
Fax: (615) 213-4426
Email:
inquiry@lightningsource.com
https://www.lightningsource.com

(UK)
Lightning Source UK Ltd.
6 Precedent Drive
Rooksley
Milton Keynes
MK13 8PR, UK
Email:
enquiries@lightningsource.co.uk
Voice: +44 (0) 1908 443555
Fax: +44 (0) 1908 443594

Library of Congress Control Number: 2004091849

Schansberg, Christopher R.
Reasons to Believe: Evidence for the Christian Message
ISBN 0-9729754-7-0

"Jesus said, 'If anyone is thirsty, let him come to me and drink."
(John 7:37)

To Lee Schansberg, the love of my life
To Sarah and Katie – God's precious gifts

Contents

Acknowledgements _____ 1

Introduction _____ 3

Is The Bible Historically Reliable? _____ 5

Did Jesus Defeat Death? _____ 27

Understanding Jesus Christ _____ 46

Don't All Religions Lead To God? _____ 55

The Universal Sense of Guilt _____ 61

The Debate about the Origins of the Universe ____ 67

Some Important Questions _____ 75

In the Final Analysis _____ 84

Works Referenced or Recommended _____ 86

Acknowledgements

I have heard it said a book is the result of a group effort. Based on the experience of writing this book, I would have to agree. Without the help of so many, this book would not have been possible.

I must first thank my wife, Lee, for sacrificing the time and energy it took to help in the writing of this book. Thank you for listening to my many ideas, critiquing and encouraging as appropriate. The Bible says, "*a prudent wife is from the Lord.*" Indeed! Thank you also to my daughters, Sarah and Katie – your lives inspire me "more than you know."

I wish also to thank the fellowship of Dauphin Island Baptist Church. Without their support, this book – and some of the more wonderful moments of the last six years – would not have been possible. I appreciate the privilege of growing spiritually and relationally with all the members of the congregation. Much appreciation should be expressed to Jerry Waller for his reading (and rereading) and correcting of this manuscript. I also appreciate Edith Roberts and her efforts in typing up my original lecture notes, which served as the foundation of this book.

I also appreciate the ongoing support of my family. I wish to say thank you to Lee's parents, Jim and Mae Shaw, for their support of this project and for their continuing love. I also appreciate the enriching role my brother, Eric Schansberg, has played to my ministry over the years – "*couldn't have done it without ya!*" Thank you also to my sister, Cathy Schansberg, for her encouragement. I wish to express my appreciation to my grandma, Esther Weller, whose faith has greatly strengthened me through the years. I am also grateful to my parents, David and Sandra Schansberg, for their interest in this project and the gift of their love.

Finally, I wish to express my appreciation to Larry Wilson whose vision made this book possible.

      Chris Schansberg
      February 2, 2004

Introduction

Paul said, "*I speak frankly, for I am sure these events are all familiar to him, for they were not done in a corner! King Agrippa, do you believe the prophets? I know you do...*"

"*Agrippa said to Paul, 'Do you think that in such a short time you can persuade me to be a Christian?' Paul replied, 'Short time or long – I pray God that not only you but all who are listening to me today may become what I am [a Christian]...'*" (Acts 26:26-29)

From its beginning, the Christian message has been a message of hope based on reliable evidence. It is the purpose of this book to provide some of this evidence in a brief and compelling form. My own interest in this subject began when I was in my early teen years. After having made a decision for Christ, I began to ask if my decision was based in facts or wishful thinking. After twenty years of exploring the historical, philosophical and scientific claims of the Christian message, I have found it to be sound in every way. I expect this book to help the reader in discovering the soundness of the Christian message as I have.

The purpose of this book is to lay the groundwork for a serious commitment to Jesus Christ. In my years of ministry, I have often found people make an initial commitment to Christ without understanding the profundity of the commitment they have made. Further, people often discuss the Christian message without a clear understanding of the solid historical and intellectual foundation upon which it stands. It is my hope this book will serve to give a summary understanding of the Christian message and the intellectual integrity of such a commitment.

       Chris Schansberg
       February 2, 2004

Chapter One
Is The Bible Historically Reliable?

The foundation of the Christian message is the Bible. Before someone is willing to consider the Bible as a source of authority in their lives, the first question asked might be, "Can I know the Bible's story is true?" This is a good question. The Bible claims to be a history of God's working in the lives of those who choose to surrender their lives to his leadership. Therefore, the basic question of the story's reliability needs to be asked.

To answer this question, some of the basic aspects of the composition of the Bible need to be addressed. To begin with, the Bible is divided into the "Old Testament" and the "New Testament."[1] Both the Old and New Testaments were written as a series of separate documents (called *books*, *gospels* or *letters*). The first seventeen books of the Old Testament are a written history of God's work among the people of Israel. The next five books of the Old Testament are called *Wisdom* writings. They include advice for daily living (*Proverbs* and *Ecclesiastes*) and songs of worship (*Psalms*). These books also include books that tackle the subject of romance (*Song of Songs*) and the question of suffering (*Job*). The last seventeen books of the Old Testament are the collected works of prominent prophets (preachers) throughout the history of Israel.

The first four books of the New Testament are called *gospels*. A *gospel* is a biography of Jesus' life, which focuses on his ministry, death and resurrection. The next book, *Acts*, is a history of the early Christian movement. The next books of the New Testament are *epistles*. Written by prominent leaders in the early church, the *epistles* were written to help the reader learn how to understand and live out her life in the modern world. The last book of the New Testament, *Revelation*, is a letter from the Apostle John sharing a vision he experienced. In this vision, Jesus spoke about how the world would end.

We will take three approaches to establishing the reliability of the historical accounts related in the Old and the New Testaments. First, we will consider whether we have accurate records of what the Biblical writers originally wrote. Second, we will consider whether the historical accounts given in the Bible are confirmed by extra Biblical historical studies. Third, we will explore the style of writing of the Biblical documents and ask if the writing style adds or detracts from their credibility.

THE BOOKS OF THE BIBLE

Old Testament *History*	Old Testament *The Prophets*	New Testament *Gospels*	New Testament *Epistles*
Genesis	Isaiah	Matthew	1 Peter
Exodus	Jeremiah	Mark	2 Peter
Leviticus	Lamentations	Luke	1 John
Numbers	Ezekiel	John	2 John
Deuteronomy	Daniel		3 John
Joshua	Hosea	*History*	Jude
Judges	Joes	Acts	
Ruth	Amos		*Prophecy*
1 Samuel	Obadiah	*Epistles*	Revelation
2 Samuel	Jonah	Romans	
1 Kings	Micah	1 Corinthians	
2 Kings	Nahum	2 Corinthians	
1 Chronicles	Habakkuk	Galatians	
2 Chronicles	Zephaniah	Ephesians	
Ezra	Haggai	Philippians	
Nehemiah	Zechariah	Colossians	
Esther	Malachi	1 Thessalonians	
		2 Thessalonians	
Wisdom		1 Timothy	
Job		2 Timothy	
Psalms		Titus	
Proverbs		Philemon	
Ecclesiastes		Hebrews	
Song of Songs		James	

THE OLD TESTAMENT
Textual Accuracy – Do we have an Accurate Record of What the Old Testament Writers Originally Wrote?

The Bible claims to be written by many different authors – among who were national leaders, poets, prophets, tax collectors, fishermen and in one case a former terrorist. A basic question often asked is "do we have an accurate record of what these persons originally wrote?" This is a legitimate and important question.

An investigation of the Old Testament documents shows the answer to be a ringing "Yes!" We can know with certainty we have in our Bibles an accurate copy of what the authors of the Old Testament documents wrote.

Each of the Biblical documents began with an initial document – called the "autograph" – penned by the author. This autograph document would serve to be the basis of all following documents. From this point, the document would be hand copied by succeeding generations of copyists. This process continued unabated until the advent of the printing press in the 15th Century (A.D.).

Today there are over ten thousand of these copies of the Old Testament books written in the Hebrew language.[2] These copies were written between the third century B.C. and the fourteenth century A.D.

When these texts are compared with each other, they are in word for word agreement 95 percent of the time.[3] This is astonishing! Imagine how many opportunities for mistakes there were in the process of hand copying over a period of hundreds, even thousands, of years. Yet for all this, there is only a 5 percent degree of error. The story gets even more interesting when you consider the majority of these errors are comprised of slips of the pen, grammatical and spelling errors that are easily detected. Of the errors left, none significantly influences the meaning of the text or Christian beliefs.[4] This high degree of agreement of the texts guarantees we have accurate copies of the writings of the Old Testament authors.

How could these copyists have duplicated the Old Testament texts over thousands of years, with such a degree of accuracy? Today we know of some of the practices of the copyists – and the degree of effort they put into their work is, to say the least, astonishing.

For instance, Samuel Davidson reports on the copying practices of the Jewish scholars called the Talmudists (A.D. 100-500).

Davidson reports the rolls[5] used for copying were to be of the hides of certain animals, prepared specifically for the use of copying the scriptures. Every hide was to contain a certain number of columns, equal throughout the entire roll. Further, every column was to be between forty eight to sixty lines. When finished, the copies were checked for letter for letter accuracy and the spaces between letters and paragraphs were to be according to a uniform code. Additionally, Davidson reports the color of the ink (black) was regulated.[6]

Bible scholar, F.F. Bruce reports on the copying practices of the Jewish scholars called the Masoretes (A.D. 500-950). Bruce states the Masoretes were disciplined to a great degree and protected the text with the "*greatest imaginable reverence, and devised a complicated system of safeguards against scribal slips. They counted, for example, the number of times each letter of the alphabet occurs in each book; they pointed out the middle letter of the Pentateuch and the middle letter of the whole Hebrew Bible, and made even more detailed calculations than these. (Bruce then quotes Wheeler Robinson): "everything countable seems to be counted..."*[7]

The Jewish people regarded the Old Testament text as sacred – as being literally the words of the living God. Their high regard for the sacred nature of the Old Testament drove them to seek word for word accuracy in copying the texts – believing to alter the text in any way was a sin against God. Proverbs 30:6 (from the Old Testament) says, "*Do not add to his [God's] words, or he will rebuke you and prove you a liar.*" The respect of the Jewish people for the Old Testament accounts for why we have accurate copies of what the Old Testament writers originally wrote.

Is the Old Testament Historically Accurate?
The next question we consider is whether the historical reporting given in the Old Testament is confirmed by historical evidence. Why is this important? If we can give evidence for the historical reliability of the Old Testament then we are closer to being able to trust its claim to represent the very words of God.

The Account of Jericho (Joshua 2:1-6:27)
One of the examples of the Old Testament's historical accuracy is seen in the remarkable similarity between the findings of

modern archaeologists and the Biblical accounts of Jericho's demise. The story of Jericho's demise is told in Joshua 2:1-6:27. According to the Biblical account:
- A strongly fortified city (Jericho) is attacked by the people of Israel.
- The attack occurred just after harvest time in the spring.
- The city was a short siege of the city, in which the walls were leveled and burned.
- The claim of the Biblical text that the city was not plundered.

These details are confirmed in amazing specificity by the archaeological record.[8]

The Location and Destruction of Sodom and Gomorrah (Genesis 13:10-12, 19:23-26, 28)
The Bible states Sodom and Gomorrah were in a group of five cities found in the area of what is now the Dead Sea. The Bible tells us the cities of Sodom and Gomorrah were destroyed in a fiery conflagration because of their disobedience to God.

Until the advent of recent discoveries, skeptical researchers had questioned the Bible's story of Sodom and Gomorrah's location and destruction. Archaeological evidence now reveals all five of the cities mentioned in the Bible were in fact centers of commerce in the area. Further, evidence of intense heat, burning, earthquake and other geological disturbance reveals the area was subject to the violent upheaval described in the Biblical text.[9]

The Price Paid for Joseph
The Bible says Joseph, one of the patriarchs of the people of Israel, was sold into slavery for twenty shekels of silver (*Genesis 37:28*). Archaeological studies have now confirmed this is indeed the correct price for the period represented by the book of Genesis. K.A. Kitchen says, "*Earlier than this, slaves were cheaper (10-15 shekels), later than this, more expensive.*"[10]

Joseph's Burial Arrangements
Joseph eventually rose from slavery, to become the second in command to the King of Egypt. Toward the end of his life, the Bible states Joseph requested the people of Israel take his body with them when they would leave Egypt (*Genesis 50:24-26*). The Bible records how Moses honored this wish, and took

Joseph's body with the Israelites when they left Egypt (*Exodus 13:19*). The Bible also records how Joshua, Moses' successor, did finally bury Joseph's body within Israel's borders in the town of Shechem (*Joshua 24:32*).

For centuries, there was a tomb at Shechem venerated as the tomb of Joseph. When the tomb was opened, a body was discovered which had been mummified according to Egyptian burial customs and in the tomb was a sword of the type worn by Egyptian officials of Joseph's time.[11]

Sennacherib's Siege of Jerusalem (2 Kings 18:17-19:37, Isaiah 36:1-37:38)
The Bible tells of the King of Assyria's (Sennacherib) siege of Jerusalem during the reign of King Hezekiah. The Bible records how Sennacherib was able to capture all of the cities of Hezekiah except the city of Jerusalem. Archaeological excavations of the Assyrian palace of Ashurbanipal have now found Sennacherib's own version of the events – complete with his own "spin" of his failure to capture Jerusalem.

> "*As to Hezekiah, the Jew, he did not submit to my yoke. I laid siege to 46 of his strong cities, walled forts, and to the countless small villages in their vicinity...I drove out of them 200,150 people, young and old, male and female, horses, mules, donkeys, camels, big and small cattle beyond counting and considered (them) booty. Himself I made a prisoner in Jerusalem, his royal residence, like a bird in a cage.*"[12]

The Bible also tells of the assassination of Sennacherib by two of his sons (*2 Kings 19:37, Isaiah 37:38*). Assyrian records confirm the accuracy of this account as well.[13]

Old Testament Cities, Towns and Nations
Throughout the Old Testament, towns and nations in the region of Israel are frequently mentioned. Today many of these ancient towns and nations have been identified – just as the Old Testament names them. No contradiction has been found in the Bible's naming and locating of various cities, towns and nations and the findings of modern historical research.[14]

Chapter One: Is The Bible Historically Reliable?

Foreign Kings
Twenty six foreign kings (non Israelite) are named in the Old Testament. When compared with archaeological records we find each of these king's names is reproduced with complete phonetic accuracy in the Old Testament text. In addition, all kings are listed properly in regard to their chronological place in history.[15]

Old Testament Words – Anachronisms or Not?
In the early part of the twentieth century, some scholars charged that the Old Testament text was full of anachronisms – that it used words that could not have come from the time frame represented by the text. For example, if a letter was found that appeared to be written by Abraham Lincoln, historians would check for the presence of anachronisms. If it were found to include the phrase, "*I [Lincoln] forgot to shut off my personal computer,*" it would be recognized as a forgery because personal computers came into existence long after Lincoln.

Biblical scholars now conclude the words and phrases employed throughout the Old Testament text are accurate to the timeframes represented by the individual writers.[16]

The Straightforward Reporting of Facts
One method for determining whether a document is historically reliable is to look at its treatment of its subject. Does the writer's style communicate he is serious about writing a historical account? Does the writer shade the truth or does the writer "lay it out" without playing favorites? When confronted with this type of analysis, the Old Testament once again demonstrates we can trust its historical accuracy.

On the issue of style, the writers of the Old Testament repeatedly make clear that accuracy is one of their central goals. The Old Testament is primarily a history of the people of Israel designed to recount the special working of God in their midst. For this reason, accuracy in the accounts was treasured by its writers.

Consider the efforts of the writer of Genesis to make clear that one famine he is referring to is not confused with another. *Genesis 26:1* says, "*Now there was a famine in the land— besides the earlier famine of Abraham's time—and Isaac went to Abimelech king of the Philistines in Gerar.*"

There is also the account of the Exodus of the people of Israel from Egypt. In the following section, notice the precise attention given to details about avoiding the region of the Philistines and even the roads taken. Why include such detail if you are not interested in accurate history? Exodus 13:17-18, "*When Pharaoh let the people go, God did not lead them on the road through the Philistine country, though was shorter. For God said, "If they face war, they might change their minds and return to Egypt." So God led the people around by the desert road toward the Red Sea*"

There are also the frequent notes referring to other historical works "for further research." Such as the note in *1 Kings 11:41*, "*As for the other events of Solomon's reign—all he did and the wisdom he displayed—are they not written in the book of the annals of Solomon?*" Notice also Isaiah's concern to note the times in which he prophesied. *Isaiah 1:1* says, "*The vision concerning Judah and Jerusalem Isaiah son of Amoz saw during the reigns of Uzziah, Jotham, Ahaz and Hezekiah, kings of Judah.*"

This book could be filled alone with references such as these. The evidence shows the Old Testament writers clearly had a concern to report history accurately.

Did the writers "shade the truth" in favor of the heroes of the Bible? This would not be an uncommon practice for this day and time – as official historians routinely distorted their reports to make their nation and leaders look good. Yet this is not what we see in the Old Testament. The writers of Old Testament history spell out the character faults of Biblical heroes just as clearly as their strengths.

Abraham
Abraham was considered the Father of the entire nation of Israel. Yet while the Bible clearly records his great faith, his generosity and his bravery, the Bible also records his unfortunate habit of lying and of compromise when the situation suited him.

Moses
Consider the uncomplimentary record of Moses' life. Although the high points of his accomplishments are recorded – so are his low points. The Biblical text clearly records Moses' committing of

murder and his difficulty in controlling his temper throughout his life.

David
David's reign was considered the pinnacle of success for the nation of Israel. Yet along with David's moments of triumph, the Bible tells about his adulterous affair with Bathsheba and of David's murder of Bathsheba's husband.

The People of Israel
Most official histories tend to put the national record in a good light. Yet the Bible unhesitatingly records the many failures and sins of the people of Israel as well as their successes. The Bible records the exact reason for the downfall of the nation – their refusal to obey God and his ultimate judgment on the nation.

When the writing style of the Old Testament is analyzed, we have more than enough reasons to trust the writers were indeed making a serious effort to record accurate history.

When Were the Old Testament Books Written and Who Wrote Them?
People often wonder when the books of the Bible were written and who their true authors were. Until recently, it was commonly believed the books of the Bible were written in the time frame claimed by the book in question. The question of who wrote each book was determined by comments of the writers of the Biblical text. Where this means of identification is not available, the authorship of the text has been left open to question.

For instance, the opening words of the Book of Jeremiah are "*The words of Jeremiah son of Hilkiah, one of the priests at Anathoth in the territory of Benjamin.*"[17] Clearly, this text is representing itself as a record of the words of Jeremiah, the ancient Old Testament prophet (preacher).

This perspective on the authorship and date of writing of the Old Testament books has been called into question in the popular media by a number of scholars. The traditional understanding of the authorship and dating of the Old Testament books has been challenged – ultimately undermining popular acceptance of the historical reliability of the Old Testament books.

Do the Old Testament books authentically represent the writings of individuals who were inspired by God, or are they elaborate forgeries? This question can be answered when we consider the overall historical accuracy of the Old Testament books. We know from our study of the Old Testament that every indicator points its historical soundness. Based on this knowledge, we can ask, *why question the Old Testament's claims of authorship?"* No sufficient reason can be found to doubt the Old Testament's various claims to authorship. Therefore, it is only reasonable to conclude the books of the Old Testament were written by the writers claimed within the Old Testament texts.[18]

Conclusion – Is the Old Testament Historically Accurate?
In conclusion, we know we have accurate copies of what the Old Testament writers originally wrote. We also know the Old Testament writers reported history accurately. Finally, we know the Old Testament writers wrote in a straightforward manner designed to communicate history accurately. Based on this we conclude the Old Testament is in fact historically accurate.

THE NEW TESTAMENT
Textual Accuracy – Do We Have an Accurate Record of What the New Testament Writers Originally Wrote?
If the case for the preservation of the original words of the Old Testament authors is strong, the case for the New Testament is overwhelming. Today we can say with absolute certainty we have an accurate record of what the New Testament authors wrote.

AUTHORS AND APPROXIMATE DATING OF THE OLD TESTAMENT BOOKS[19]

Genesis – *Moses, 1500 B.C. – 1250 B.C.*
Exodus – *Moses, 1500 B.C. – 1250 B.C.*
Leviticus – *Moses, 1500 B.C. – 1250 B.C.*
Numbers – *Moses, 1500 B.C. – 1250 B.C.*
Deuteronomy – *Moses, 1500 B.C. – 1250 B.C.*
Joshua – *Joshua, 1200 B.C.*
Job – *unknown, unknown B.C.*
Psalms – *King David, various, 1250 B.C. – 500 B.C.*
Proverbs – *King Solomon, various, 962 B.C. – 922 B.C.*
Ecclesiastes – *King Solomon, 962 B.C. – 922 B.C.*
Song of Songs – *King Solomon, 962 B.C. – 922 B.C.*
Isaiah – *Isaiah, 745 B.C. – 680 B.C.*

Judges – *Samuel, 1200 B.C. – 1020 B.C.*
Ruth – unknown, *1200 B.C. – 1020 B.C.*
1 Samuel – *Samuel, 1200 B.C. – 1020 B.C.*
2 Samuel – *Samuel, 1200 B.C. – 1020 B.C.*
1 Kings – unknown, *1000 B.C. – 400 B.C.*
2 Kings – unknown, *1000 B.C. – 400 B.C.*
1 Chronicles – *possibly Ezra, 1000 B.C. – 400 B.C.*
2 Chronicles – *possibly Ezra, 1000 B.C. – 400 B.C.*
Ezra – *Ezra, 450 B.C.*
Nehemiah – *Ezra, 425 B.C.*
Esther – unknown, *450 B.C. – 350 B.C.*
Jeremiah – *Jeremiah, 627 B.C. – 560 B.C.*
Lamentations – *Jeremiah, 627 B.C. – 560 B.C.*
Ezekiel – *Ezekiel, 600 B.C.*
Daniel – *Daniel, 580 B.C.*
Hosea – *Hosea, 788 B.C. – 725 B.C.*
Joel – *Joel, 400 B.C.*
Amos – *Amos, 775 B.C.*
Obadiah – *Obadiah, 586 B.C.*
Jonah – *Jonah, 800 B.C.*
Micah – *Micah, 730 B.C.*
Nahum – *Nahum, 630 B.C.*
Habakkuk – *Habakkuk, 615 B.C.*
Zephaniah – *Zephaniah, 480 B.C.*
Haggai – *Haggai, 480 B.C.*
Zechariah – *Zechariah, 480 B.C.*
Malachi – *Malachi, - 450 B.C.- 400 B.C.*

The process of writing, recording, and preserving the New Testament is very similar to the processes used for the Old Testament. Each book of the New Testament began as an original "autograph." In turn, this autograph was duplicated repeatedly over the course of many years. Today we have 5,686 Partial and complete copies of the New Testament in Greek (the language in which the New Testament was written) written between 127 A.D. – 1400 A.D.[20]

In addition to these copies, we have 24,000 plus copies of the New Testament in other languages (Latin Vulgate, Ethiopic, Slavic, Armenian and other languages).[21] Additionally we have the resource of 36,289 quotes of the New Testament from various sources in the second to fourth centuries. (We could reconstruct the entire New Testament alone from these sources, minus 11 verses!)[22]

From these 65,000 plus texts, we can reconstruct the entire New Testament text with 99.5% accuracy.[23] The majority of the remaining .5% is mainly misspellings, grammatical mix-ups, or slips of the pen.[24] In all cases, no doctrine of Christianity is put in question by any text in question. New Testament Scholar David Dockery states, "*Although there are certainly differences in many of the New Testament manuscripts, not one fundamental doctrine of the Christian faith rests on a disputed reading.*"[25]

To reassure us further we can look at the dates of the copies of the New Testament manuscripts we possess. In many cases, these copies are dated within hundreds of years and in some cases within decades of the original writing of the New Testament documents.[26]

Importance of the Agreement of the Biblical texts with Each Other
Why is the agreement between copies of the Old or New Testament a guarantee we have an accurate copy of what the Biblical authors wrote? Allow me to explain by creating a hypothetical example. Let's take, for instance, the gospel of Luke. The gospel of Luke was written approximately 60 A.D. (approximately 30 years after Jesus' death and resurrection). The writer of Luke wrote the gospel of Luke and the book of Acts and then sent them on to the intended recipient - Theophilus (see *Luke 1:1-4* and *Acts 1:1*). As with all ancient books there would have been only one original document, as people in those days could not generate multiple manuscripts when writing an article or book as we can today.

Luke would send his original work to Theophilus. Theophilus, in turn, would have shared the document with his church. If the document helped them in understanding the Christian message, they would make copies of the *Gospel of Luke* and the *Book of Acts* to share with other churches. Those churches would then receive them and, if they liked what they had read, make more copies and pass them on to other churches. It's not too difficult to see how a mistake could work its way into this growing group of copies (and copies of copies). If a copyist were to leave out any part of the manuscript, all copies based on this copy would be inaccurate. Very soon, we would have an easily detectable pattern of inconsistencies within the pool of New Testament texts.

Chapter One: Is The Bible Historically Reliable?   17

The amazing thing is while it would not be too difficult to imagine how a mistake could work its way into this process, it never actually did! As with their Jewish predecessors, those who copied the New Testament and passed them on to others considered those texts sacred. Therefore, they sought to copy with the greatest possible accuracy. Even keeping in mind human diligence, one must seriously consider the idea God miraculously watched over the copying of the New Testament and safeguarded the accuracy of the texts.

Comparing the New Testament to Other Popular Ancient Works
When you compare the manuscript accuracy of the New Testament with other popular ancient manuscripts, we see other ancient books are not as well authenticated by their resources. Bruce Metzger estimates the *Mahabharata* of Hinduism is copied with 90% accuracy, Homer's *Iliad* with 95% accuracy.[27]

Josh McDowell also points out the number of manuscripts by which to verify other ancient texts are much less than the New Testament resources. For instance, the *Iliad*, written by Homer, was written in 800 B.C. and has 643 manuscripts to verify its accuracy. The earliest copy is dated at 400 B.C. (a time gap of 400 years between the writing of the book and the earliest surviving copy).

The *Histories*, by Herodotus, written 480-425 B.C., has 8 manuscripts by which to verify its accuracy. The earliest copy is dated at 900 A.D. (a time gap of 1,350 years between the writing of the Histories and the earliest surviving copy).

Plato's writings, written in 400 B.C., have 7 manuscripts to verify its accuracy with the earliest copy dated at 900 A.D. (a time gap of 1,300 years between the writings of Plato and the earliest copies we have).

Caesar's *Gallic Wars*, written between 100-44 B.C. has 10 manuscripts by which to verify its accuracy with the earliest dated copy at 900 A.D. (approximately a 1000 year gap between the writing of *Gallic Wars* and the earliest surviving copy).

The accuracy of these well known texts is rarely questioned. Yet the New Testament's accuracy is often questioned – despite the overwhelming amount of evidence that we have accurate copies of what the original authors wrote (dated within *two hundred years* and even *decades* of the original writings).[28]

Historical Accuracy – Is the New Testament Historically Accurate?

As with the Old Testament, the archaeological record confirms the historical accuracy of the New Testament to a very great degree. In fact, it can be said such ample evidence exists today that we know with certainty the New Testament text is historically accurate and reliable.

John's Five Covered Colonnades (John 5:2)
In *John 5:2*, the gospel writer specifically says in Jerusalem there was a pool near the Sheep Gate. The writer of John specifically states this pool had five covered colonnades. (A colonnade is a series of columns supporting the base of a roof structure). It is interesting the writer makes this as an offhand remark. He is claiming to have been well acquainted with the city of Jerusalem. Excavations of this area of Jerusalem have now been done and they have discovered the site John spoke of – with five colonnades![29]

In Which Province Does the City of Iconia Belong? (Acts 14:1-6)
In *Acts 14:1-6*, the writer speaks of the Apostle Paul traveling to three cities within the jurisdiction of Rome – Lystra, Derbe and Iconia. In this passage, the writer states cities of Lystra and Derbe are located within the province of Lycaonia. The writer then implies the city of Iconia is outside this province.

In the nineteenth century, it was thought this account was in error. This was because of writings of other contemporaries of the author of Acts, which stated Iconia was part of the province of Lycaonia. In the end, however, the writer of Acts was discovered to be correct. The cities in question (Lystra, Derbe and Iconia) were part of the region of Galatia, which was subdivided into four provinces: Isauria, Pisidia, Phrygia and Lycaonia. Although Iconia was generally considered part of the province of Lycaonia, during the years 37 A.D. – 72 A.D., (the period claimed to be represented in this section of Acts), Iconia was removed from Lycaonia's sphere, and put under the authority of the province of Phrygia due to various political considerations.[30]

It is significant to note the detail of accuracy seen in this passage. Again, this is an almost offhand remark – but it demonstrates the seriousness with which the writer of Acts approached the question of historical accuracy.

Countries, Cities and Islands Reported in the Book of Acts
The writer of Acts claims to be a person who lived in the times he writes about, and to have experienced many of the events as well. We would expect such a person to be able to give accurate reporting about the areas through which he claims to have traveled. This is indeed the case. Dr. Norman Geisler reports the writer of Acts names thirty two countries, fifty four cities, and nine islands all with 100% accuracy.[31]

Erastus, Director of Public Works (Romans 16:23)
In *Romans 16:23* the Apostle Paul writes from the city of Corinth, "*Erastus, who is the city's director of public works, and our brother Quartus send you their greetings.*" The existence of Erastus was confirmed during the excavations of Corinth in 1929 when this inscription was found on a section of pavement. "*Erastus, curator of public buildings, laid this pavement at his own expense.*"[32]

F.F. Bruce states, "*The evidence indicates this pavement existed in the first century A.D., and it is most probable the donor is identical with the Erastus who is mentioned by Paul.*"[33]

The Seven Churches of Revelation (Revelation 2:1-3:21)
The book of Revelation has often been the focus of much speculation about the future. Its record of historical accuracy, however, should not be overlooked! In the early chapters of Revelation, detailed mention is given of seven cities and their churches. Each of the references to these cities provides valuable historical detail about these cities. For example, the members of the church of Laodicea are encouraged to "*salve to put on your eyes, so you can see.*"[34] Historians have discovered the city of Laodicea was famous for producing an eye ointment with great healing properties. There are many such instances like this throughout the book of Revelation.[35]

These are just a few of the historical facts supporting the New Testament story. The historical accuracy of the New Testament is the rule, not the exception.

The Straightforward Reporting of Facts

As with the Old Testament, the New Testament must be probed to discover whether its writers intended to report history soberly and accurately. The intent of the writer is of utmost concern. For instance, if the writer of a particular work intended to write a fiction than we would know we should not bother to rely on their work as a history.[36] By contrast, if the intent of a writer was to report history accurately, than we would know we could consider their work as being a possible source of accurate history.

The New Testament is well supplied with references to the intent of the writers to relay accurate historical information. The following examples are a sampling of such statements in the New Testament.

The Writer of Luke and Acts
The person who wrote the gospel of Luke and the book of Acts clearly states he was trying to communicate history accurately and fairly. *Luke 1:3-4* states, "*Therefore, since I myself have carefully investigated everything from the beginning, it seemed good also to me to write an orderly account for you, most excellent Theophilus, so you may know the certainty of the things you have been taught.*"

Peter's Account
In the time of the New Testament writers, it was common for people to produce fictitious histories and try to pass them off as historical accounts. Peter, trying to make it clear what he was talking about was not made up, states, "*We did not follow cleverly invented stories when we told you about the power and coming of our Lord Jesus Christ, but we were eyewitnesses of his majesty.*" (*2 Peter 1:16*)

The Apostle John
Throughout the Apostle John's gospel and letters, the historical nature of the reporting is constantly reaffirmed. Consider *John 21:24*, "*This is the disciple who testifies to these things and who wrote them down. We know that his testimony is true.*" John himself testifies in *1 John 1:1-3*, "*The one who existed from the beginning is the one we have heard and seen. We saw him with our own eyes and touched him with our own hands. He is Jesus Christ, the Word of life. This one who is life from God was shown to us, and we have seen him. And now we testify and*

announce to you that he is the one who is eternal life. He was with the Father, and then he was shown to us. We are telling you about what we ourselves have actually seen and heard...." (NLV)

That the New Testament writers were attempting to report accurate history cannot be denied. This forces us to treat the accounts of the New Testament writers as being – at the very least – serious attempts to report historical facts.

In our study of the Old Testament, we discovered a bias or lack of bias shown toward the subject can help us to determine the reliability of a historical report. In addition, we should consider if the writer tries to hide faults within the people and events portrayed. Again, we will see the New Testament reports the straight facts and avoids glossing over embarrassing or difficult truths.

Unflattering Portrayal of the Disciples
One of the constant themes throughout the gospels is the repeated failure of the Disciples – the twelve closest friends of Jesus – to understand him or follow his teaching. Repeatedly the disciples show an inability to understand Jesus' message of peace and love towards their fellow neighbor, and seem constantly on a quest for personal power. Only after Jesus' resurrection do the disciples "get it." Yet why would the writers of the gospel portray the future leaders of the new church as so incompetent at understanding their master's message?

The Prominence of Women
An additional perspective on the straightforward nature of the New Testament's reporting is seen in how it highlights the role and value of women in the life of Jesus and the early church. The New Testament repeatedly highlights women in prominent roles and even states they were the first eyewitnesses to the resurrection. This is curious when one considers the lack of respect in which women were held in that time. Women were seen to have little credibility as either leaders or witnesses in a legal setting. From the perspective of the New Testament writers, the decision to introduce women so prominently in their reporting would have greatly reduced the chances of their writings being accepted. Why report this unless it was true?

Accepting the Unaccepted
Another curious aspect of the reporting of the New Testament is the tendency to highlight those whom society rejected. Repeatedly throughout the New Testament the poor, the sick, the weak, and the old are portrayed as being central players in the work of Jesus. Today we accept this perspective. In the society in which the New Testament was written, however, such persons were seen as worthless. Why report this unless it was true?

When Were the New Testament Books Written and Who Wrote Them?

When the New Testament writings were written and who wrote these documents has recently been brought into question by scholars in the popular media. Until recently, the accepted belief was the New Testament was written by the persons represented by the text. It was also believed the New Testament writings were written in the timeframes represented by the writings themselves.

How are the identities of the New Testament writers determined? Usually the name of the writer is determined from cues within the text. For example, the epistle (letter) to the Romans clearly states it was written by Paul the apostle. *"Paul, called to be an apostle of Christ Jesus by the will of God, and our brother Sosthenes, to the church of God in Corinth."*[37] In instances where the name of the New Testament writer is not clearly stated, historical sources outside the Biblical record may be used to supply the names of the person who authored the text. This is the case in the gospels of *Matthew, Mark, Luke, John* and the book of *Hebrews*. The timeframes in which the New Testament writings were written are also determined from cues within the text.

As with the Old Testament, some scholars challenge the authorship and date presumed by the Biblical record. Are these challenges valid? At first, these challenges often seem to present a challenge to the Biblical record. Detailed study, however, vindicates the accepted names of the authors and the dates of writing.

We can use the data we have studied to draw our own conclusions. In our study, we have seen the historical accuracy of the text demonstrated repeatedly. In addition, we know from the straightforward style of writing of the New Testament there is no hint of favoritism in its reporting. The historical accuracy of the New Testament and the straightforward style of writing are important because they help us to discern forged historical accounts from genuine historical accounts.

An example of a forged historical account can be seen in the *Gospel of Peter* – discovered in 1889, in Upper Egypt.[38] This document, claiming to be written by Simon Peter, gives a very interesting account of the resurrection event – to say the least! In this account, Jesus' resurrection is witnessed by the guards at the tomb and the religious leadership who executed Jesus. In the course of events, two angels as tall as the sky exit the tomb holding the hand of another – presumably Jesus – whose head reaches taller than the sky. If this isn't enough, the angels and Jesus are followed by a talking cross.[39] Obviously, the writer of the *Gospel of Peter* was not interested in reporting history accurately, and he clearly was not above adding his own poetic embellishments.

AUTHORS AND APPROXIMATE DATING OF THE NEW TESTAMENT BOOKS[40]

New Testament Gospels[41]
Matthew – *Matthew*, 65 A.D. – 72 A.D.*
Mark – *Mark*, 64 A.D.*
Luke – *Luke*, 69 A.D.*
John – *John*, 65 A.D. – 90 A.D.*

History
Acts – *Luke*, 69 A.D.*

Epistles
Romans – *Paul, 57 A.D.*
1 Corinthians – *Paul, 54-56 A.D.*
2 Corinthians – *Paul, 54-56 A.D.*
Galatians – *Paul, 48 A.D.*
Ephesians – *Paul, 60 A.D.*
Philippians – *Paul, 60 A.D.*

New Testament Epistles
Colossians – *Paul, 60 A.D.*
1 Thessalonians – *Paul, 50 A.D.*
2 Thessalonians – *Paul, 50 A.D.*
1 Timothy – *Paul, 63-65 A.D.*
2 Timothy – *Paul, 63-65 A.D.*
Titus – *Paul, 63-65 A.D.*
Philemon – *Paul, 63-65 A.D.*
Hebrews – *unknown, 68 A.D.*
James – *James, 58 A.D.*
1 Peter – *Peter, 67 A.D.*
2 Peter – *Peter, 67 A.D.*
1 John – *John, 90 A.D.*
2 John – *John, 90 A.D.*
3 John – *John, 90 A.D.*
Jude – *Jude, 82 A.D.*

	Prophecy
* indicates when an author's name is derived from historical sources and not directly from the Biblical text.	Revelation – *John*, 90 A.D.

By contrast, note the sparseness of the record and the lack of embellishment when the gospels report about the miracles or the resurrection of Jesus. Notice how they simply report the event, and leave the audience to draw their own conclusions.
Can we trust the New Testament claims about the authorship and times of writing of its various books? Yes, we can!

Conclusion
When we compare the textual accuracy, the historical accuracy and the style of writing of the New Testament, we conclude the New Testament is historically accurate. Once this is decided, we are forced to consider the issues addressed by the New Testament. These issues include the claims of Jesus, his miracles and his resurrection – which we will investigate in the following chapters.

---

[1] The word "Testament" means "covenant" or "contract." This word is rarely seen today except in reference to legal documents – for instance, a person may refer to his will as his "last will and testament." The term "Old Testament" (or contract), refers to the contract God offered humanity before Jesus came. The term "New Testament" (or contract) is used to refer to the new contract God now offers humanity through Jesus.
[2] McDowell, Josh D. *The New Evidence that Demands a Verdict.* Nashville, Tennessee: Thomas Nelson Publishers, 1999. p. 69-90.
[3] Geisler, Norman L.. *"Old Testament Manuscripts."* Baker Encyclopedia of Christian Apologetics. Grand Rapids, Michigan: Baker Books, 1999. p. 553.
[4] Ibid., p. 553.
[5] In this time, writing was done on rolls of parchment or similar material, instead of the sheets of paper we use today.
[6] Davidson, Samuel. The *Hebrew Text of the Old Testament.* p. 89. As quoted from McDowell, Josh D. *The New Evidence that Demands a Verdict.* p. 74.
[7] Bruce, F.F. *The Books and the Parchments: How We Got Our English Bible.* Old Tappan, New Jersey: Fleming H. Revell Co. 1950. p. 117. As quoted from McDowell, Josh D. *The New Evidence that Demands a Verdict.* p. 75.

[8] Wood, Bryant G. "Did the Israelites Conquer Jericho?" *Biblical Archaeology Review*. March / April 1990. pp. 44-59. As quoted from McDowell, Josh D. *The New Evidence that Demands a Verdict*. p. 95.
[9] Geisler, Norman L.. *"Archaeology, Old Testament."* Baker Encyclopedia of Christian Apologetics. p. 50-51.
[10] Kitchen, K.A. The Ancient Orient and the Old Testament. Chicago, Illinois: InterVarsity Press. 1966. pp. 52-53. As quoted from *The New Evidence that Demands a Verdict*. p. 108.
[11] Elder, John. Prophets, Idols and Diggers. New York: Bobbs Merril Co. 1960. p. 54. As quoted from *The New Evidence that Demands a Verdict*, 1999. p. 110.
[12] Pritchard, James B. ed. *The Ancient Near East, vol. 2. A New Anthoogy of Texts and Pictures*. Princeton, New Jersey: Princeton University Press. 1975. p. 52. As quoted in Geisler, Norman L.. *"Archaeology, Old Testament."* Baker Encyclopedia of Christian Apologetics. p. 52.
[13] Watts, John D.W. *Scene 4: A Reading (continued): Isaiah's Response from Yahweh (37:21-38) Comment – v. 38*. Isaiah 34–66, Volume 25, Word Biblical Commentary, Dallas, Texas: Word Books, Publisher, 1987.
[14] Kitchen, K.A. *The Bible in its World*. Downers Grove, Illinois: InterVarsity Press, 1978. pp. 53-54. As quoted from *The New Evidence that Demands a Verdict*. pp. 101-102.
[15] Wilson, Robert Dick. A Scientific Investigation of the Old Testament. Chicago, Illinois: Moody Press. 1959. pp. 64, 71. As quoted from McDowell, Josh D. *The New Evidence that Demands a Verdict*. p. 70.
[16] Kitchen, K.A. *The Bible in its World*. Downers Grove, Illinois: InterVarsity Press, 1978. p. 50. As quoted from *The New Evidence that Demands a Verdict*, 1999. pp. 101-102.
[17] *Jeremiah 1:1*.
[18] For a more detailed exploration of these issues, please see: McDowell, Josh D. *The New Evidence that Demands a Verdict*.
[19] The dates given are based in great part on the following article. Butler, Trent C., editor. *"Timeline."* Holman Bible Dictionary. Nashville, Tennessee: Holman Bible Publishers, 1991.
[20] Strobel, Lee. *The Case for Christ*. Grand Rapids, Michigan: Zondervan Publishing House. 1998. p. 63.
[21] Ibid., p. 63.
[22] McDowell, Josh D. *The New Evidence that Demands a Verdict*. Nashville, Tennessee: Thomas Nelson Publishers, 1999. p. 43.
[23] Strobel, Lee. *The Case for Christ*. p. 65.
[24] Geisler, Norman L.. *"New Testament Manuscripts."* Baker Encyclopedia of Christian Apologetics. p. 532.
[25] Dockery, David. Foundations for Biblical Interpetation. Nashville, Tennessee: Broadman and Holman Publishers, 1994. p. 182. As quoted from McDowell, Josh D. *The New Evidence that Demands a Verdict*. p. 35.

[26] McDowell, Josh D. *The New Evidence that Demands a Verdict.* p. 38.
[27] Geisler, Norman L.. *"New Testament Manuscripts."* Baker Encyclopedia of Christian Apologetics. pp. 532-533.
[28] McDowell, Josh D. *The New Evidence that Demands a Verdict.* p. 38.
[29] Beasley-Murray, John George R. *"II. The Public Ministry of Jesus, Sub Section C. Jesus the Mediator of Life and Judgment (4:43–5:47) Notes – note: g."* Gospel of John, Volume 36, Word Biblical Commentary. Dallas, Texas: Word Books, Publisher, 1987.
[30] Fernando, Ajith. The NIV Application Commentary. Grand Rapids, Michigan: Zondervan Publishing House. pp. 24-25.
[31] Geisler, Norman L.. *"Archaeology, New Testament."* Baker Encyclopedia of Christian Apologetics. 1999. p. 64.
[32] Bruce, F.F. *The New Testament Documents: Are They Reliable?* Downers Grove, Illinois: InterVarsity Press. 1981. p. 96.
[33] Ibid., p. 96.
[34] Revelation 3:18.
[35] Barclay, William. *The Revelation of John, volume 1.* The Daily Study Bible Series. Philadelphia, Pennsylvania: Westminster Press. 1976. pp. 138-139.
[36] Of course, we could use a fictitious work to determine a number of historical facts. One example of this would be to see what type of reading material was popular in the time in which the work was written. However, the genre of writing – in this example, fiction – would keep us from taking the work as a record of history.
[37] *Romans 1:1-2.*
[38] Miller, Robert J., editor. *The Complete Gospels – Annotated Scholars Version.* San Francisco, California: HarperCollins, 1994. p. 399.
[39] Miller, Robert J., editor. *The Complete Gospels – Annotated Scholars Version.* p. 403.
[40] The dates in this table are based on the following article (except where noted). Butler, Trent C., editor. *"Timeline."* Holman Bible Dictionary.
[41] The dating of the gospels, *Acts* and Paul's epistles are based, in part, on the work of F.F. Bruce. Bruce, F.F. *The New Testament Documents: Are They Reliable?* pp. 4-15.

Chapter Two
Did Jesus Defeat Death?

The Bible states Jesus died by crucifixion – one of the most horrible means of death ever devised by the human race. The victim of crucifixion died due to a number of factors such as blood loss, exposure, asphyxiation, exhaustion and other causes. The Bible asserts Jesus also went through exhausting physical and emotional ordeals immediately prior to his crucifixion.

To become familiar with Jesus' ordeals and crucifixion please read: Matthew 26:46-27:56, Mark 14:43-15:41, Luke 22:47-23:49 or John 18:1-19:37.

The Bible makes many radical claims. One such claim is Jesus defeated death and bodily rose from the dead. The authority of the Christian message relies on the historical reality of the resurrection of Jesus. If Jesus was not resurrected, than the Christian message is invalid. If he was resurrected from the dead, than the Christian story is true and everyone should treat its news with the utmost respect. The Apostle Paul wrote, "*...if Christ has not been raised, our preaching is useless and so is your faith*" (*1 Corinthians 15:14*).

Before discussing whether Jesus' resurrection occurred, we need to be clear about what the Christian story claims the resurrection to be. In our day, it is a trend to redefine key terms in order to reconcile various points of view. At times, this approach to dialogue has merit. In the case of discussing the Christian claim, however, we must be clear what the New Testament writers meant when they stated Jesus Christ was resurrected from the dead.

DEFINING WHAT "RESURRECTION" MEANS
First, resurrection is not the survival of death in a ghost like state. In myth and popular media, a ghost is supposed to be a person's soul or spirit in a disembodied state. Jesus said, "*Look at my hands and my feet. It is I myself! Touch me and see; a ghost does not have flesh and bones, as you see I have*" (*Luke 24:39*).

Resurrection cannot properly be defined as a resuscitation of one's body. While this captures part of the definition of resurrection, it fails to take seriously the concept of transformation. The Bible says not only was Jesus brought back from death (as was Lazarus, see *John 11*), but his body was transformed.

The New Testament concept of resurrection defies eastern religious concepts as well. The claim of the resurrection is not a claim of reincarnation. Reincarnation is defined as the rebirth of a soul in a new mortal human body – usually with a new identity for the person reincarnated. Jesus' resurrection body is immortal and he clearly retained his sense of self identity.

Resurrection cannot be defined as the attaining of enlightenment, *Nirvana*, *satori* or *moksha*. These terms imply the loss of a person's identity as he merges with God as a drop of water absorbs into the ocean. Jesus clearly remained an embodied individual.

Jesus' resurrection was not translation or assumption into heaven. This Jewish concept is seen in the translation / assumption of Enoch and Elijah in the Old Testament. This concept is different from the resurrection, in part, because it is the idea of a person being taken from earth to heaven. Resurrection is the idea of Jesus' return from the realm of the dead to the earth.

Some understand Jesus' resurrection as a vision experienced by the disciples. A vision is an experience occurring to an individual as an internally experienced event (in one's mind). It is internally processed and cannot be externally verified, as it has no reality except to the observer. Jesus resurrection body was clearly more than this. Jesus was touched by those he appeared to, he ate in their presence and he was seen by many people at the same time.

Neither is the resurrection a myth or legend. Myths and legends are, by definition, non historical events. They are based in the imaginations of the persons who create them. The early church clearly claimed the resurrection as an objective, verifiable event in human history.

Chapter Two: Did Jesus Defeat Death?

Finally, Jesus' resurrection is not the *"triumph of Easter faith in the hearts and lives of the disciples."*[1] This perspective claims the stories of the miracles serve as encouragement to the Christian to live charitable and good lives even though the resurrection (and other miracles) did not happen as objective events in history. This idea is completely foreign to the New Testament as it is essentially an act of self deception. Faith needs to have an object or person on which it rests. According to the New Testament perspective, if Jesus did not bodily rise from the grave then faith is a waste of time and an illusion.[2]

What the Resurrection Is
If it is important to define what the resurrection is not, it is important to define what it is. The Bible says the resurrection is the beginning of a new order of things that will not be completed until the time of Jesus' return. It is the intrusion of the spiritual world – which we consider as transient and unreal – into the physical world – which we think is permanent. The result of this intrusion is a transformation of both spiritual and physical realities into something new. Paul calls this "something new" by different terms – *"first fruits," "the last Adam," "the clothing of the perishable with the imperishable,"* and *"the spiritual body."*[3] The resurrection is not only the resuscitation of a corpse, but the implanting of a new power within that body. This power transforms and raises the human body to the highest possible levels of life – God's life. Interestingly, Jesus promised he was not the only one who would experience this resurrection life, but so will all who receive him as their Lord and Savior.[4]

DID JESUS DEFEAT DEATH?
Since we now know what the New Testament means by "resurrection," we can now ask an important question. The question is, *can we know with certainty that Jesus Christ was resurrected from the dead*? In the exploration of this question in the next pages, I believe you will discover we can confidently know Jesus indeed defeated death through his resurrection.

Modern scholars – Christian and skeptic alike – believe certain key elements of the resurrection story are beyond any doubt. These key elements are as follows:
    1. Jesus died by crucifixion.
    2. Jesus was buried.

3. Jesus' disciples were devastated by his death and had no real hope for the future.
4. Jesus' tomb was discovered to be empty just a few days later.
5. Jesus' disciples experienced what they believed were actual appearances of the resurrected Jesus.
6. Jesus disciples were radically changed by their post death experiences of Jesus to such an extent they were willing to eventually die for their proclamation of his resurrection.
7. James, Jesus' brother (who previously did not support his brother's radical claims) believed he saw the resurrected Jesus and was converted.
8. Paul, a persecutor of early Christians, was converted by an experience he believed to be an encounter with the resurrected Jesus.
9. The Christian church was founded by these disciples.
10. The primary day of Christian worship was moved from Saturday to Sunday, the day on which Jesus was reported to have risen.[5]

Some of the elements of the above outline will be reviewed more thoroughly in the pages to come. This outline establishes the basic elements of the resurrection story that are universally agreed upon as historical fact.

To answer the question of whether Jesus resurrected, I want to use a simple outline to help us thoroughly explore all of the possible answers to the question. This outline begins with a question – *what happened to Jesus' body after he died?*

What Happened to Jesus' Body?

The New Testament records Jesus' body was taken from the cross and buried in a Palestinian tomb. As with any burial, there are two possibilities as to what happened to Jesus' body – either it remained in the tomb or it did not.

If Jesus' body remained in the tomb, we must account for the behavior of Jesus' disciples and their opponents. Why would Jesus' disciples proclaim the resurrection story if it did not occur? Further, if Jesus' body remained in the tomb, one must ask why the authorities did not produce the decomposing body of Jesus to counter the claim of the resurrection event.

On the other hand, if Jesus body departed the tomb, we must attempt to discover how it left. Did it leave through the actions of an outside party or did Jesus' body leave the tomb under its own power?

Possibility One: The Body Remained in the Tomb
In our investigation, we will first explore the way events usually unfold for people who are buried – let's suppose Jesus' body remained in the tomb. If this was the case, it puts the "fault" of proclaiming Jesus' resurrection squarely on the shoulders of Jesus' disciples as they proclaimed Jesus had risen from the dead. There are only two ways to account for such an apparently false course of action – either the disciples proclaimed Jesus' resurrection knowing they were lying; or, the disciples themselves were somehow fooled into thinking Jesus was alive.

WERE THE FOLLOWERS OF JESUS LYING?
The idea of the followers of Jesus lying about Jesus' resurrection encounters a number of substantial difficulties. The first question would have to be simply, *why would they lie about such a thing*? There are a many reasons this is unlikely. First, there is the simple fact of the reverence they had for Jesus. Despite their frequent misunderstandings of Jesus, his followers clearly believed he was the coming Messiah of Jewish hope. As such, Jesus' followers were depending on him for the deliverance of their nation from Roman oppression and for their own personal blessing as well. His death cut short those hopes. What strange turn of heart would cause his followers to react to this tragedy in such a way?

We also must account for the cooperation of Jesus' mother and brothers in this charade. The New Testament lists them as witnesses of the resurrection and followers of Jesus. It is important to note the devotion of Jesus' family to his message comes after his death.[6] Before Jesus' death, his family neither understood him nor supported his ministry.

There is the further challenge of the price the apostles paid for their proclamation of the resurrection of Jesus. History tells us Jesus' closest followers – the inner group of the eleven apostles – faced many difficulties and died difficult deaths because of their proclamation of Jesus' resurrection. In spite of the difficulties they endured, there is no record of an apostle ever renouncing the proclamation of the resurrection. The apostles would spend the rest of their lives living and preaching an ethic of self sacrifice and service to other people. What lie could account for their sacrifice?

There is the challenge presented by the first witnesses of the resurrection – a group of women who had gone to the tomb to anoint Jesus' body for burial. The accounts of the women in the gospels are considered by almost all New Testament scholars as accurate. Why are these stories held in such high regard? In Jesus' day, the testimony of women was considered worthless. It is reasoned no one would report such a story unless it was true. The idea of inventing a story in which women were the first witnesses would be viewed as counterproductive in that time. If the disciples lied about Jesus' resurrection, it is unimaginable they would create the story of the women's discovery of the empty tomb as it would severely undermine their claims!

We must reckon with the conversion of Paul. Before Paul became a Christian, he considered the suppression of the Christian message and church to be an item of top priority for him and all faithful Jewish persons. Yet this all changed when Paul saw the resurrected Jesus! (For one account of his story, see *Acts 9:1-30*).

Finally, the religious and secular leaders would have only needed to go to Jesus' tomb and produce his corpse to show such a lie for what it was. Of course, if the disciples had decided to lie about Jesus' resurrection, they might have considered stealing the body and hiding it. (To consider this possibility, see *Did the Disciples Steal the Body?* in the next section, *Jesus' Body Exited the Tomb*).

The disciples did not lie about the resurrection of Jesus. Instead, our review demonstrates the disciples were being honest and truthful when they claimed to have seen the resurrected Jesus.

WERE THE DISCIPLES VICTIMS OF A HOAX?
Even though the disciples' were honest about their claim to have seen the resurrected Jesus, this does not exclude the possibility they were *honestly mistaken*. Perhaps the disciples were the

victim of a cruel hoax or some sort of delusion. In this section, we will explore these possibilities.

A reading of the gospel accounts of Jesus' death and resurrection quickly eliminate the possibility the Disciples were victims of a hoax. From all accounts, the disciples were deeply suspicious of the news of Jesus' resurrection. Each of the gospels highlights the profound initial skepticism of the disciples. It was only later that their doubt blossomed into committed belief. It was only after being presented with the reality of Jesus' resurrection in a variety of situations they came to believe Jesus was alive.

In the gospel accounts, we see the disciples experiencing a variety of supernatural events that convinced them Jesus was alive. These events included the appearance of angels to announce Jesus' resurrection, multiple experiences of Jesus appearing in their midst and Jesus' ascension to heaven. All of these experiences would have been extraordinarily difficult to counterfeit.

Consider the physicality of the post resurrection appearances of Jesus. Repeatedly we see the disciples taking hold of the risen Jesus or being invited to touch him. We also see Jesus eating with his disciples. The contact of the disciples with the resurrected Jesus was up close and personal. It would be difficult for any hoax to survive such scrutiny.

There are also the psychological aspects of Jesus' post resurrection appearances to consider. Before his death, Jesus demonstrated detailed familiarity with the details of his disciples' lives. The disciples knew Jesus as someone who knew them better than themselves. In their encounters with the resurrected Jesus, they met this same person who knew them better than themselves.

Supposing someone was able to convince the skeptical disciples Jesus had risen from the dead, there is still the question of who would perpetrate such a hoax. The religious and civil authorities would certainly not, because they wanted this problem to go away! They certainly did not want Jesus' disciples thinking their leader was alive. The idea of other persons attempting this is not reasonable either. Jesus had just been crucified by the authority of the Roman Government. The penalties for such folly would likewise be extreme.

Therefore, we conclude the disciples were not the victims of a hoax.

WERE THE DISCIPLES THE VICTIMS OF A HALLUCINATION?
Some believe the disciples were the victims of a hallucination. It is suggested because the disciples wished Jesus to be alive they convinced themselves they had seen him. This theory, however, does not stand upon close examination of the facts.

Hallucinations are private, individual and internally experienced events. In contrast to this, the majority of recorded post resurrection appearances are to groups of people. One group numbered over five hundred people (*1 Corinthians 15:6*).

Hallucinations are experienced under certain limited conditions of either mindset or situation. By contrast, the post resurrection appearances of Jesus occurred under a variety of circumstances. Jesus appeared to his disciples privately and when they were together in groups. He appeared to them when they were at both leisure and work. Jesus appeared to his disciples when they were in different frames of mind – moments of grief, moments of confusion (over the issue of his resurrection) and moments when they were full of hope.

Another problem with this theory is one of simple credibility. If you were to see a dead man walking and talking, wouldn't you think you were hallucinating or at least needed to see the eye doctor? It is only reasonable to expect the same of the disciples. Remember, the initial reaction of the disciples to the news of the resurrection was disbelief. *Matthew 28:17* gives a summary statement of the disciples' reaction to seeing Jesus after his resurrection. *"When they saw him, they worshiped him; but some doubted."*

Consider these other difficulties with the hallucination theory.
1. Hallucinations are usually fleeting experiences – Jesus appeared over the course of forty days.
2. Hallucinations cannot be touched and they do not eat. The New Testament says the disciples touched Jesus

Chapter Two: Did Jesus Defeat Death?

and he ate real food to prove he was not a figment of their imagination.

3. Hallucinations don't hold profound and meaningful conversations. Yet Jesus conversed with his disciples on a variety of subjects ranging from personal to political issues. For one such conversation, see *John 21:15-23*.
4. On three occasions (*Luke 24:13-31, John 20:15, 21:4*), the disciples who saw Jesus failed to recognize him. If the disciples had been hallucinating, you would think they could identify their own hallucination!
5. People hallucinate along the lines of what is already known or believed. The concept of resurrection was an entirely new concept among Judaism and other world religions. If the resurrection appearances were the result of the imaginations of the disciples then they most likely would have been interpreted as a *translation* or *assumption into heaven* (please see: *Defining what "Resurrection" Means,* above). These interpretations would have been more in line with Jewish beliefs of the time.
6. The New Testament records two people – James, the brother of Jesus, and Saul – who were converted when they saw the risen Christ. "... *[Jesus] appeared to James...and last of all he appeared to me [Paul]...*"[7] Before their conversions, James and Paul were both hostile to the Christian message. James and Paul could not have been the victims of a hallucination because they had no emotional need to see Jesus.

Finally, if the friends of Jesus had all hallucinated, they would not have had a reason to disturb the body. As a result, when the disciples began to proclaim Jesus had risen from the dead, the religious and civil leaders would have simply produced Jesus' corpse and put an end to the Christian movement before it gained significant momentum.

Consequently, we know the hallucination theory is not a satisfactory explanation of the resurrection event.

No other explanations account for the actions of the disciples and the possibility the body of Jesus remained in the tomb. A thorough examination of the above theories reveals they do not account for the facts surrounding the resurrection event. This leads us to consider the second set of possibilities - Jesus' body exited the tomb.

Possibility Two: Jesus' Body Exited the Tomb

We conclude Jesus' body did not remain entombed but somehow exited the tomb. How could this happen? Two alternatives are open to us, either the body was removed by an outside party or Jesus departed the tomb somehow alive.

DID THE RELIGIOUS/CIVIL AUTHORITIES (OR BOTH) REMOVE JESUS' BODY?

We will first consider the possibility the religious / civil authorities removed Jesus' body from the tomb. This was the first guess of the disciples upon their discovery of the empty tomb. Mary Magdalene is quoted as saying, *"They have taken the Lord out of the tomb, and we don't know where they have put him!"*[8] The disciples discovered, just as we will, the idea of the authorities removing Jesus' body would not bear scrutiny.

This idea fails for many reasons. First, there is no discernable interest for the authorities to act in such a manner. While it is possible they would have removed the body to preclude the possibility of the disciples stealing Jesus' body, the historical record speaks against this. When the disciples did claim Jesus had risen from the dead, the authorities failed to produce Jesus' body to disprove the disciples' claim. In order for this idea to be true, it would imagine the authorities had Jesus' body in their possession but did not produce it when the disciples began to proclaim Jesus' resurrection from the dead!

Another reason this idea fails is because the historical record states the religious authorities had a guard posted to foil any attempt to steal Jesus' body. Why steal a body you are guarding?[9]

This idea also fails because the disciples' not only claimed the tomb was empty, but they had seen and spoken to Jesus! If the disciples had not personally encountered Jesus, then the empty tomb would have been a mystery to them – but they would not have proclaimed Jesus' resurrection.

Chapter Two: Did Jesus Defeat Death?

For these reasons, we see this theory fails to account for the resurrection event.

DID THE DISCIPLES STEAL THE BODY?

The other alternative left to us is Jesus' disciples stole his body. This idea also fails because of the many difficulties it encounters. Many of these difficulties were dealt with in a previous section (please see in this chapter, above: *Were the Disciples Lying?*)

The psychological challenges to this hypothesis are enormous. Under what conditions could we conceive of Jesus' family and friends being convinced to desecrate the body by removing it?

Even if we grant the disciples and the family of Jesus the psychological ability to overcome the normal feelings one has for the remains of a deceased loved one they would have had to contend with the Roman guard stationed at the tomb (see Matthew 27:62-66).

The theory of the disciples stealing Jesus' body cannot account for the resurrection event.

JESUS DID NOT REALLY DIE ON THE CROSS

We have narrowed our range of possibilities so we know a third party did not remove Jesus' body. We now have to contend with the possibility Jesus survived his crucifixion and exited the tomb under his own power.

The first explanation for this possibility is one that supposes Jesus did not die on the cross. This theory suggests Jesus was in a coma like state resembling death when he was brought down from the cross. After Jesus was placed in the tomb, the theory continues, he revived, exited the tomb, and convinced his disciples he had risen from the dead. There are many difficulties with this theory.

The Roman soldiers responsible for his crucifixion were very skilled at what they did. The responsibility of insuring Jesus' death fell to them. Had Jesus escaped death, the soldiers knew very well they would pay for such dereliction of duty with their lives. The New Testament account plainly says the soldiers inspected Jesus' body and declared him dead.[10]

One detail of the soldier's inspection was to thrust a spear into Jesus' chest to guarantee he was dead. The New Testament account tells us when the soldier thrust the spear into Jesus' side it brought forward a "*sudden flow of blood and water.*"[11] The appearance of blood and water is a good medical indication death had already occurred.[12] According to an article in the *Journal of the American Medical Association* if Jesus had not been dead at this point, the spear thrust would have most likely killed him by perforating not only the right lung but also the pericardium and heart.[13]

The second difficulty is the interest Pilate, the Roman governor who had sentenced Jesus to death, took in the matter. The Gospel of Mark gives the account of Pilate's interest in the situation. "*Joseph of Arimathea...went boldly to Pilate and asked for Jesus' body. Pilate was surprised to hear that he was already dead. Summoning the centurion, he asked him if Jesus had already died. When he learned from the centurion that it was so, he gave the body to Joseph.*"[14] With the Roman Governor's interest focused on the issue, we may be sure Jesus' executioners made sure of his death.

The third difficulty is the grave clothes in which Jesus' body was wrapped before his burial. They would have made impossible an escape from the tomb. The grave clothes were wrapped in the fashion of an adhesive bandage around the body. In addition, they were coated in seventy five pounds of embalming spices (*John 19:39-40*). These spices acted as a glue or cement to hold the wrappings together and they created a solid covering. Jesus, weakened as he was by his crucifixion ordeal, would have been unable to escape the grave clothes – or even breathe through them.

There are other difficulties to account for. Consider the following:
- The New Testament record, in accordance with burial practices of the time, recounts Jesus' tomb was sealed by rolling a large stone across the entrance. (Small caves were often used as tombs. A stone, set in a groove, was rolled across the entrance). How could Jesus have rolled aside the stone from the inside?[15]
- The New Testament account also records the authorities had posted guards outside his tomb. (In the event

Chapter Two: Did Jesus Defeat Death?

Jesus' disciples would try to steal Jesus' body and fulfill his prediction of his own resurrection[16]). How could Jesus, in his weakened state, have overpowered the guard outside the tomb?
- The New Testament relates an account of two of Jesus' disciples in which Jesus walked with them from the city of Jerusalem to Emmaus (a seven mile walk). Shortly after, Jesus appears to the disciples in Jerusalem (a seven mile walk back to town)! How would it be possible for Jesus to walk fourteen miles when he had experienced the driving of iron spikes through his feet and ankles during his crucifixion three days earlier?
- How would Jesus have convinced his skeptical disciples he was the Risen Lord of Life, and not just a sick and injured man?

Perhaps the most overwhelming objection to this theory is the very character of Jesus himself. Would Jesus, who preached the need for truth, integrity and love, have lied in such a way? For these reasons, we find this theory cannot account for the resurrection event.

JESUS WAS BODILY RESURRECTED BY THE POWER OF GOD
We conclude Jesus' body left the tomb and it did not exit the tomb by the methods that would commonly account for such an event. How then did Jesus' body exit the tomb? We are left with one possible answer, the answer of the Bible – God raised Jesus from the dead. There are ten reasons to take this possibility seriously.

1. Overwhelming Eyewitness Testimony.
The historical record of the New Testament gives us impressive and unimpeachable accounts Jesus rose from the dead. The eyewitness accounts of the risen Jesus provided to us come from poor and rich, educated and uneducated. They come from individuals and groups. Their experiences of the risen Jesus occurred in a variety of circumstances and emotional states over a forty day period. In spite of the initial skepticism of the witnesses, they were won over by the fact of Jesus' transformed and living body – right in front of them. The Apostle Peter's words on this matter are to the point, "*God has raised this Jesus to life, and we are all witnesses of the fact.*"[17] (For some of the other accounts of the resurrection, read the final chapter of the

Gospels of *Matthew*, *Mark* and *Luke*, the last two chapters of the *Gospel of John*, the first two chapters of *Acts*, and *1 Corinthians 15:3-8*).

Of course, it may be objected these events occurred long ago – and so how can we know they happened? From our earlier chapter, *Is the Bible Historically Reliable*, we know of the historical reliability of the Bible. So while these events occurred long ago, we know we have reliable records of these events.

2. Jesus' Prediction of His Resurrection and His Post Resurrection Statements.
Another reason to trust the story of the resurrection event is Jesus himself predicted he would rise from the dead. Consider these passages.

Jesus said, "*...A wicked and adulterous generation asks for a miraculous sign! But none will be given it except the sign of the prophet Jonah. For as Jonah was three days and three nights in the belly of a huge fish, so the Son of Man will be three days and three nights in the heart of the earth.*"[18]

"*Jesus answered them, "Destroy this temple, and I will raise it again in three days."...the temple he had spoken of was his body.*"[19]

"*[Jesus] told them, "This is what is written: The Christ will suffer and rise from the dead on the third day, and repentance and forgiveness of sins will be preached in his name to all nations, beginning at Jerusalem.*"[20]

Jesus expected to defeat death – and he did!

3. The Changed Attitude of the Disciples.
When Jesus was arrested by the religious authorities, his disciples abandoned him. After Jesus' death, the disciples were utterly demoralized and went into hiding. After the resurrection event, however, the disciples are fearless in the face of the authorities and all threats. What can account for this change? The disciples accounted for it by explaining they had seen the risen Jesus, they knew he was Lord of all, and so they did not need to fear. Acts 4:13 says, "*When they [the religious leadership] saw the courage of Peter and John and realized that*

they were unschooled, ordinary men, they were astonished and they took note that these men had been with Jesus." To learn more about the adventures and boldness of the disciples, read the book of *Acts* in the New Testament.

4. The Conversion of James.
Before the resurrection event, James is not listed as a follower of Jesus and apparently opposed his ministry. After the resurrection event, James is listed among the disciples and becomes a prominent leader in the church. What can account for this change? The only satisfactory explanation is the one given by the New Testament: Jesus appeared to his step-brother. As a result, James became convinced Jesus is Lord.

5. The Conversion of Paul.
Before his conversion to Christianity, Paul was a terrorist who delighted in capturing, imprisoning and even killing Christians. Paul viewed the Christian message as a threat and blasphemy. Yet, Paul became a Christian and a prominent leader in the Christian movement. Why the change? He said it was because he had seen the resurrected Jesus.[21]

6. Sunday as a Day of Worship and Rest.
The founders of the early church were Jewish. As persons of Jewish belief and background, they believed the seventh day (Saturday) was to be set aside as a day of worship and rest. Yet very early in Christian history Sunday became the day of worship and rest. What can attest to this change in a practice that had been observed by the Jewish people for centuries? The only satisfactory reason available is the one given in the New Testament – Sunday became the day of worship, rest and celebration because it was the day on which Jesus rose from the dead.[22]

7. The Fact of the Empty Tomb.
Jesus' burial in the tomb of Joseph of Arimathea and the empty tomb are established facts.[23] How can the empty tomb be explained? As we reviewed in the various theories above, no explanation outside the resurrection event is able to explain these facts adequately.

8. The Existence of the Christian Church.
If Jesus did not rise from the dead then the existence of the Christian Church must be explained. The New Testament records the first founders of the Christian movement were men and women who claimed to have seen the risen Jesus. If not for their work, the Church would not have come into existence. Apart from the resurrection of Jesus, the existence of the institution of the Christian Church cannot be accounted for.

9. The Millions Who Have Encountered His Living Presence.
The New Testament states Jesus is alive. Christianity is not founded upon an idea or philosophy but upon the claim that individual people can have a relationship with Jesus Christ. Since the resurrection event, when people call on the name of Jesus they find they encounter a real person. Of course, this is not the same as physically seeing Jesus as some of the early followers of Jesus did. Yet millions of people - in many cultures and nations - have attested to a powerful encounter with the living Jesus that has changed their lives.

10. The Best Explanation for the Cumulative Evidence.
The case for Jesus' resurrection is compelling not only because of the individual lines of evidence listed above, but also because of the cumulative effect of the evidence. The only convincing explanation of all of the facts is Jesus' resurrection.

Conclusion – Jesus is Risen From the Dead!
When all the possible facts and perspectives are considered, there is only one reasonable conclusion to make: *Jesus is risen from the dead*! If Jesus rose from the dead, this validates the many claims he made about himself. In the next chapter, we will consider these claims and explore what bearing they have on our lives.

Dealing with Differences in the Resurrection Accounts
A reading of the accounts of the resurrection event in the New Testament will demonstrate there is a striking unity in the overall story presented. All of the accounts testify to a basic outline of facts – Jesus rose from the dead, the first witnesses of the resurrection were women and Jesus then appeared to a number of other witnesses. On the other hand, when compared with each other, these reports also have differences in the details reported. Some accounts report the appearance of one angel,

Chapter Two: Did Jesus Defeat Death?

where other accounts report the appearance of several angels. One account speaks of a group of women going to Jesus' tomb, while another speaks of one woman. What are we to make of these differences? Do they add to or subtract from the credibility of their reports? Are these differences complimentary or contradictory?

There are three possible perspectives one can hold in regard to the different versions of the resurrection event reported in the New Testament.

    1. The differences in the accounts point to a lack of historical accuracy in the New Testament accounts. Therefore, it is concluded, the accounts cannot be trusted and the possibility of Jesus' resurrection is not taken seriously.

    2. The differences in the accounts of the resurrection event point to the overall reliability of the account of the resurrection event. When criminal investigators question witnesses, they expect minor differences in the accounts of the people questioned. This is a mark the witnesses have not colluded on their stories.

    This approach accepts the overall credibility of the reports of the resurrection event, without straining at minor details. For this approach, the bodily resurrection of Jesus and other details of the accounts are accepted – the first witnesses of the resurrection event being women, the various experiences of the disciples, etc. Minor details of the accounts, such as the number of angels actually present at the tomb and other variations are actually viewed as strengthening our regard of the historical reliability of the resurrection accounts.

    3. The differences in the accounts of the resurrection event emphasize the extreme accuracy that characterizes the Bible. In this approach, the differences seen in the accounts of the resurrection events are the result of the reporting of minute details by various witnesses.

Because of our understanding of the overall historical reliability of the Bible, the first approach – rejecting the resurrection story because of differences in the accounts – can be summarily discarded. Few modern scholars would seriously suggest the gospel accounts are not accurately recorded history. Whatever conclusions we may draw, this approach is not available to us.

If the New Testament accounts of the resurrection event are correct in the major details than the overall integrity of the Christian message does not suffer. We still know the resurrection event occurred and we must consider Jesus' message seriously.

If, on the other hand, the New Testament accounts are accurate in every detail, than what seem at first to be contradictions in the historical accounts are found to be complimentary details. Of course, if this approach is correct than the resurrection event is also demonstrated to have occurred.

Having read the Bible for over two decades, I (the writer) have struggled with the question of which of the last two approaches best fits the New Testament data. While either approach supports the Christian story, I find the third approach listed above best fits all the information we posses. Comparing the details of each of the resurrection accounts, I have found they compliment each other to a great degree. In the end, however, whether the reports of the resurrection event are accurate in general or in all of their details is an irrelevant question. We know as a matter of historical fact Jesus defeated death and bodily rose from the dead. This leads us to the next chapter.

---

[1] Kreeft, Peter and Tacelli, Ronald K. *Handbook of Christian Apologetics*. Downers Grove, Illinois: InterVarsity Press, 1991. p. 181.
[2] Much of my outline comes from Kreeft, Peter and Tacelli, Ronald K. *Handbook of Christian Apologetics*. pp. 178-181.
[3] see 1 Corinthians 15:1-56.
[4] see John 3:16, 5:24-29, 6:39-40.
[5] Based on the outline from, Habermas, Gary R. and J.P. Moreland. *Beyond Death: Exploring the Evidence for Immortality*. Wheaton, Illinois: Crossway Books, 1998. p. 113.
[6] Jesus' mother and brothers are listed as being witnesses of the resurrection despite their early resistance to his mission and message – see *Mark 3:21, Luke 8:19-21, John 7:5, Acts 1:14* and *1 Corinthians 9:5*.

[7] *1 Corinthians 15:7-8.*
[8] *John 20:2*
[9] The authorities tried to keep Jesus' body in the grave instead of removing it! See *Matthew 27:62-66.*
[10] For more details, read *John 19:31-36.*
[11] *John 19:34.*
[12] Edwards, William D., Gabel, Wesley J., Hosmer, Floyd E. *On The Physical Death Of Jesus Christ.* Journal of the American Medical Association. Vol. 255 No. 11, pp. 1397-1488, March 21, 1986.
[13] Edwards, William D., Gabel, Wesley J., Hosmer, Floyd E. *On The Physical Death Of Jesus Christ.*
[14] *Mark 15:43-45.*
[15] McDowell, Josh D. *The New Evidence that Demands a Verdict.* Nashville, Tennessee: Thomas Nelson Publishers, 1999. pp. 230-231.
[16] *Matthew 27:62-66.*
[17] *Acts 2:32.*
[18] *Matthew 12:39-40.*
[19] *John 2:19, 21.*
[20] *Luke 24:46-47.*
[21] *1 Corinthians 9:1* – "Have I not seen Jesus our Lord?"
[22] *Exodus 20:8-11, Luke 24:1, Acts 20:7, 1 Corinthians 16:2.*
[23] See: Craig, William Lane and Ludeman, Gerd. Copan, Paul and Tacelli, Ronald K. editors. *Jesus' Resurrection – Fact or Figment?* Downers Grove, Illinois: InterVarsity Press, 2000. pp. 162-206.

Chapter 3
Understanding Jesus Christ

In the 1990's a popular song asked a poignant question, *"What if God were one of us?"*[1] This song expressed the seemingly eternal desire of humanity to connect with God. It speaks of the aching yearning of humanity for God to meet us on our terms – becoming like us to communicate with us. When we look to Jesus, we find these longings answered in him. Consider these quotes from the Bible:

> *"She [Mary, Jesus' mother] will give birth to a son, and you are to give him the name Jesus, because he will save his people from their sins." All this took place to fulfill what the Lord had said through the prophet: 'The virgin will be with child and will give birth to a son, and they will call him Immanuel'—which means, 'God with us.'" (Matthew 1:21-23)*

> *"In the beginning was the Word [a title for Jesus], and the Word was with God, and the Word was God. He was with God in the beginning. Through him all things were made; without him nothing was made that has been made...The Word became flesh and made his dwelling among us. We have seen his glory, the glory of the One and Only, who came from the Father, full of grace and truth." (John 1:1-3, 14)*

> *"For God so loved the world that he gave his one and only Son, that whoever believes in him shall not perish but have eternal life." (John 3:16)*

In summary, the Bible tells us Jesus is the Son of God, who became a man, so he could bring both God and humanity together. The Bible declares, *"For there is one God and one mediator between God and men, the man Christ Jesus..."* (1 Timothy 2:5)

Jesus – the Son of God
In becoming familiar with Jesus, we find ourselves involved in the mystery of what it means for him to be the Son of God. The

mystery deepens when we consider the Bible teaches there is only one God. "*This is what the* LORD *says— Israel's King and Redeemer, the* LORD *Almighty: I am the first and I am the last; apart from me there is no God.*" (*Isaiah 44:6*).[2] If there is only one God, how could Jesus be the Son of God?

The Bible explains this by proclaiming God is *one God in three persons.*[3] The Bible reveals God as Father, Son (Jesus) and Holy Spirit. This does not mean God uses the concept of Father, Son and Holy Spirit to express himself. On the other hand, this does not mean there are three Gods. God is one being, yet three persons. Each of these persons is both equally and eternally God.[4] Of course, this is radically different from the human experience, as a human is one being and one person. Nevertheless, the Bible says God is greater than we can comprehend. We should not be surprised when we do not fully understand him!

In each of these passages the Father (God), Jesus and the Holy Spirit are spoken of as being equal with God and as being the same as God.

> *"Therefore go and make disciples of all nations, baptizing them in the name of the Father and of the Son and of the Holy Spirit..." (Matthew 28:19)*
>
> *"For the one whom God has sent speaks the words of God, for God gives the Spirit without limit. The Father loves the Son and has placed everything in his hands." (John 3:34-35)*
>
> *"You, however, are controlled not by the sinful nature but by the Spirit, if the Spirit of God lives in you. And if anyone does not have the Spirit of Christ, he does not belong to Christ. But if Christ is in you, your body is dead because of sin, yet your spirit is alive because of righteousness. And if the Spirit of him who raised Jesus from the dead is living in you, he who raised Christ from the dead will also give life to your mortal bodies through his Spirit, who lives in you." (Romans 8:9-11)*

Jesus' Self Understanding

Do we see this high view of Jesus reflected in his own words and life? Indeed we do. When we look at his life, we find the idea of being God's Son permeated all he said and did. Consider the following examples:

Jesus Claimed Authority Equal to Scripture

In Jesus' culture, the Jewish people viewed the Old Testament as being the very words of God. Jesus shared this same view of Scripture. Jesus frequently referred to the Old Testament as *"the word of God."*[5]

While Jesus shared their high view of Scripture, he held a view no observant Jew would have considered. Jesus considered his own words on the same level with Scripture. Six times in his Sermon on the Mount, he said, *"You have heard that it was said [in the Old Testament]...But I tell you"*[6] Jesus viewed himself as being able to add to the Old Testament Scriptures.

On another occasion, Jesus said, *"Heaven and earth will pass away, but my words will never pass away."* (*Matthew 24:35*) This is equivalent to what the Old Testament says about the Bible's eternally enduring nature. *"Your word, O LORD, is eternal..."* (*Psalm 119:89*)

It is worth noting Jesus' audience noticed his attitude of authority. After his Sermon on the Mount, this comment is recorded: *"When Jesus had finished saying these things, the crowds were amazed at his teaching, because he taught as one who had authority, and not as their teachers of the law."* (*Matthew 7:28-29*) Jesus taught with a unique sense of authority – he believed his words were equivalent to God's words.

Jesus Claimed his Presence Fulfilled Scripture

Another amazing aspect of Jesus' self understanding is how he saw his presence to be the fulfillment of the Old Testament writings. He believed the Old Testament was written to testify about himself.

In his inaugural sermon, Jesus preached about himself! He read a passage from the Old Testament prophet Isaiah and said, *"Today this scripture is fulfilled in your hearing."* (*Luke 4:21*) In his Sermon on the Mount, he said, *"Do not think that I have

Chapter Three: Understanding Jesus Christ

come to abolish the Law or the Prophets; I have not come to abolish them but to fulfill them." (Matthew 5:17) Once, when debating with some who opposed his message, Jesus said, *"You diligently study the Scriptures because you think that by them you possess eternal life. These are the Scriptures that testify about me..."* (John 5:39) After his resurrection, Jesus told his disciples all he had gone through was to fulfill the Old Testament writings. *"This is what I told you while I was still with you: Everything must be fulfilled that is written about me in the Law of Moses, the Prophets and the Psalms."* (Luke 24:44)

Clearly, Jesus saw himself as unique – the very fulfillment of Scripture.

Jesus Claimed Authority over the Sabbath

In Jesus' time, the Jewish people believed it was God's command they cease all work on the seventh day of the week. This day was known as the *Sabbath*. The Old Testament says, *"Remember the Sabbath day by keeping it holy. Six days you shall labor and do all your work, but the seventh day is a Sabbath to the LORD your God. On it you shall not do any work..."* (Exodus 20:8-10) The observance of this day of rest was strictly observed.

Yet when Jesus came, he claimed to have authority over the Sabbath. On one occasion, Jesus' followers were criticized for violating the Sabbath. Further, these same people criticized Jesus for not correcting his disciples. Jesus replied his disciples had done nothing wrong. Further, Jesus claimed he was the *"Lord of the Sabbath!"* (Mark 2:28) As above, his words reveal a unique sense of authority. In claiming to be Lord of the Sabbath, he was claiming to be equivalent to the one who had instituted it – God himself.

Jesus Claimed Power over the Nature, Sickness, Life and Death

Repeatedly in the Old Testament, God reveals himself as being in total control of the natural world, health, life and death.[7] Jesus viewed himself as possessing the same authority – and demonstrated the power he believed he possessed.

Jesus repeatedly verified his control over the natural world. On one occasion, Jesus and his disciples were crossing a lake in a boat. Without warning, a powerful storm appeared – threatening to sink the boat and drown all on board. Jesus had earlier fallen asleep in the stern of the boat. When events were at their worst, Jesus' disciples began to panic. It was then they came, woke him, and begged him to help. When Jesus saw the situation and their panic, he stood up and said to the storm "*Quiet! Be still!*'" (*Mark 4:39*) Immediately, the wind and waves became still.

At a wedding, Jesus demonstrated control over the processes that occur in the process of creating grapes and fermenting their juice into wine. John's gospel reports Jesus transformed water into a fine aged wine. (*John 2:1-11*)

Jesus encountered no sickness beyond his ability to cure. The Gospels report Jesus repeatedly cured a wide variety of illnesses – blindness, mental illness, deafness, and leprosy are among some of the conditions he cured. Some of the strongest authentications of Jesus' claim to be the Son of God were the miracles he performed.[8]

Jesus also demonstrated complete authority over death. Many times Jesus demonstrated his power over death by resuscitating persons who had died – in one case the person had been dead over four days.[9]

Jesus Claimed Authority to Forgave Sin
Another manner in which Jesus demonstrated his unique self understanding was how he claimed the authority to forgive sins. On one occasion, Jesus was presented with a paralyzed man. The paralyzed man's friends had taken great pains to get him to Jesus. They went to the extreme measure of digging through a roof and lowering the man through the hole – to be placed right in front of Jesus! The Bible says when Jesus saw their faith, he forgave the man of his sins. This shocked the crowd – because only God can forgive sin!

If this was a misunderstanding, Jesus could have corrected those present. He could have told them they had the wrong idea. Yet, to further the impression the crowd had of him – that he was claiming to be God – he than healed the man of his paralysis! (See *Mark 2:1-11*). This was not a unique event, as Jesus claimed the authority to forgive sins on many occasions.[10]

Jesus Claimed the Title of "Son of Man"

Jesus also claimed the special title of *"the Son of Man."*[11] This title is found in the Old Testament and is used primarily to describe two persons. On the first occasion, it is a name used for the prophet Ezekiel denoting his human frailty. The other occasion for the use of this term is in the book of *Daniel*, where it refers to a powerful individual whom God gives all power, authority and worship. *"In my vision at night I looked, and there before me was one like a son of man, coming with the clouds of heaven. He approached the Ancient of Days and was led into his presence. He was given authority, glory and sovereign power; all peoples, nations and men of every language worshiped him. His dominion is an everlasting dominion that will not pass away, and his kingdom is one that will never be destroyed."* (*Daniel 7:13-14*)

Throughout his ministry, Jesus used this unique title for himself. Repeatedly, he connects his use of the term with its usage in *Daniel 7:13-14*. One example is found in *Matthew 26:64* when Jesus said, *"Yes, it is as you say." "But I say to all of you: In the future you will see the Son of Man sitting at the right hand of the Mighty One and coming on the clouds of heaven."*[12]

Jesus Claimed to be the Son of God

Jesus also claimed to be God's Son. Today, this might be a phrase loosely used in some religious circles. *"We are all,"* it is said, *"children of God."* This would never have been said in Jesus' cultural setting. The worshipper of God was a *servant*, *slave* or at best a *friend* of God. The term *"Son of God"* was simply not used to describe one's relationship with God. Further, Jesus claimed far more than like mindedness. Jesus claimed to be the Son of God by nature as well. *"All things have been committed to me by my Father. No one knows the Son except the Father, and no one knows the Father except the Son and those to whom the Son chooses to reveal him."* (*Matthew 11:27*)

On one occasion, Jesus asked his disciples who the people thought he was. Most people were guessing Jesus was a prophet like Elijah, Jeremiah or John the Baptist. Jesus than asked his disciples who they thought he was. Peter spoke first, *"You are the Christ, the Son of the living God."* Jesus replied that Peter was right. (*Matthew 16:16-17*)

Jesus' belief that he was God's one and only son is also seen in the language he used in prayer. Before his crucifixion, Jesus, in prayer, referred to God as "*Abba.*" This is an Aramaic term which is best translated "Daddy."[13]

Jesus Claimed to be God
Jesus claimed to be God himself. As with his claim to be the Son of God, the modern person might think nothing is unusual about this. In our own society, many religions claim we are all part of God. We need to understand this idea was not part of what Jesus was communicating. The idea we are all part of God was offensive to the Jewish culture of Jesus' day. To the Jewish mind, God is utterly separate from his creatures. God is totally unique. No one in that culture would claim to be God – such words would be considered blasphemous. In claiming to be God, Jesus was claiming to be something utterly different than any other human being had ever claimed – he was the God of the Jewish people, the Lord of all creation.

In the Old Testament, God revealed his personal name to the Jewish people. This event is recorded in *Exodus 3:14.* God said his name was "*I AM.*" Jesus claimed the Hebrew name for God ("*I Am*") for himself. "'*I tell you the truth,' Jesus answered, 'before Abraham was born, I am!'*" (John 8:58)

Other examples are plentiful. Jesus said, "*I and the Father are one.*" *(John 10:30)* Jesus also said, "*If you really knew me, you would know my Father as well.*" *(John 14: 7)* Jesus equated seeing him with seeing God. "*Anyone who has seen me has seen the Father.*" *(John 14:9)*[14]

Conclusion – Jesus Understood Himself to be the Son of God
Jesus claimed to be the Son of God – a person totally unique in all of human history. That Jesus claimed to be God is a fact beyond any doubt. Either this claim was accurate, or it was not. If the claim is accurate, than Jesus has an authority unparalleled among religious teachers. If the claim is inaccurate, than everything else he said must be discounted, for that would make him either a liar or insane.

When investigated, every aspect of Jesus' life lends credibility to his unique claim. Throughout history, the unparalleled moral authority of his teachings has been recognized. Consider the

Sermon on the Mount (*Matthew 5-7*), his famous parable of the Good Samaritan (*Luke 10:25-37*), his command to love our neighbor as ourselves (*Matthew 22:39*) or his command to love our enemies (*Matthew 5:43-47*).

There is the impeccable quality of Jesus' life to consider. Jesus told us to pray for our enemies. When he was crucified Jesus prayed, "*Father, forgive them, for they do not know what they are doing.*" (*Luke 23:34*) In fulfillment of his command to love our neighbor as ourselves, Jesus continually reached out to others. Jesus did this in spite of barriers of racial prejudice, gender bias and tradition. Jesus continually ministered to people in the worst of situations and always improved the condition of the person. Jesus helped people in various types of need. These needs could include a basic need for food, offering friendship to the lonely, healing the sick, educating the ignorant, healing relationships or resuscitating the dead.

There are the miracles Jesus performed. It is important to note Jesus did not perform miracles to verify his identity as the Son of God. Instead, he performed miracles to help people in need. In spite of this, Jesus' miracles point to the truth of his claim to be the Son of God. Jesus said, "*The miracles I do in my Father's name speak for me...*" (*John 10:25*)

There is also Jesus' death to consider. The Bible tells us Jesus' death was unique for several reasons. First, Jesus claimed he would die by his own choice. His death was voluntary. "*No one takes it from me, but I lay it down of my own accord. I have authority to lay it down and authority to take it up again...*" (*John 10:18*)

Second, the Biblical record states Jesus was executed by the Roman authorities – even though he was completely innocent of all charges. The Roman governor, Pilate, said, "*As for me, I find no basis for a charge against him...*" (*John 19:6*) If there was a charge against Jesus, it was his claim to be the Son of God. (*John 19:7*)

Third, Jesus claimed his death would pay the debt every person owes to God for their sin. He said, "*...just as the Son of Man did not come to be served, but to serve, and to give his life as a ransom for many.*" (*Matthew 20:28*) "*Just as Moses lifted up the snake in the desert, so the Son of Man must be lifted up, [i.e. crucifixion] that everyone who believes in him may have eternal life." (John 3:14-15)

Finally, we must consider Jesus' resurrection. What better evidence of the truth of Jesus' claim could there be than his resurrection? Jesus said, *"No one takes it [my life] from me, but I lay it down of my own accord. I have authority to lay it down and authority to take it up again. This command I received from my Father."* (John 10:18)

Is Jesus the Son of God?
Each person must arrive at his own conclusion on this matter. Is Jesus the Son of God as he claimed to be? The evidence for Jesus' claim is overwhelming. What will you decide? Do you believe Jesus is the Son of God?

---

[1] Morissette, Alanis. *What If God Was One Of Us?* As found at: http://www.azlyrics.us/09804.
[2] For other references, see: *Deuteronomy 6:4, 2 Samuel 7:22, Isaiah 44:6, Mark 12:29, John 17:3, 1 Corinthians 8:4-6, Ephesians 4:5-6, 1 Timothy 1:17,* and *James 2:6.*
[3] Theologians refer to this threefold nature of God as "*Trinity.*"
[4] Elwell, Walter A. Evangelical Dictionary of Theology. *Trinity.* Grand Rapids, Michigan: Baker Books, 1984. pp. 1112-1113.
[5] See *Matthew 4:4, 4:10, 15:7, 22:29, 22:34-40;* and *John 10:34-36.*
[6] *Matthew 5:21, 27, 31, 33, 38* and *43.*
[7] See *Genesis 1:9-25, Psalm 103:2-5, 145:14-17;* and *1 Timothy 6:13.*
[8] See *Matthew 9:35 Mark 1:40-42,* and *Mark 10:46-52.*
[9] See *Mark 5:21-35, Luke 7:11-17,*and *John 11:1-43*
[10] See *Matthew 26:28, Luke 7:44-50, 12:10, 23:34;* and *John 20:23.*
[11] *Matthew 8:20, 9:6; Mark 14:62, John 3:14,* and *6:27.*
[12] For other references, see: *Matthew 24:27-44,* and *25:31.*
[13] *Mark 14:36.*
[14] For further references, see: *Matthew 10:40, John 8:19, 10:38,* and *12:44-45.*

Chapter 4
Don't All Religions Lead To God?

It is common to hear people assert, "*All religions lead to God.*" I am intrigued when people say this because there is no one (or very few) who really believe this statement. If questioned closely, what most people mean by this statement is "I believe *most* religions lead to God."

For example, consider the attacks on the United States that occurred September 11, 2001. These attacks were led by persons who held an extremist, militant, Islamic perspective. When the cost of that day is calculated – the lives lost, persons suffering injury, those who lost family and friends – few believe that God was pleased by the actions of these persons.

Consider the practice of human sacrifice as part of religious ritual. There are no known cases of this practice today but ritual human sacrifice has been a part of religious practice in times past. As with the September 11th Hijackers, the idea that God is somehow pleased with human sacrifice is repulsive to most. There are other, less extreme, examples. On occasion, a church or church school will be reported for taking corrective discipline to abusive levels. Often, this form of abuse is justified using religious language. There is also the abhorrent practice of female circumcision – a practice supported by some religious perspectives today.

Of course, the religious views of the September 11th hijackers cannot be said to represent the millions of followers of Islam throughout the world. Neither do the deviant religious practices of isolated groups throughout history condemn the rest of religious society. It would be a mistake to equate the various practices and beliefs of people throughout the world with these clearly abusive forms of religion.

I use these examples to point out the fact that at some point our uncritical acceptance of all religious perspectives breaks down. In truth, we do not accept all religious views. We believe religious views such as those represented above are wrong. Furthermore, we instinctively believe they offend God.

Therefore, we see while people believe most religions lead to God, it is not acceptable to think all religious views are acceptable to God. Using our own intuitive sense, we will further probe the question of which religious perspectives lead us to God, and which religions cannot. To accomplish this, I would suggest four principles based on our own experience and knowledge: (1) *the "Concern for Others" or Moral law principle*; (2) *the Self Awareness principle;* (3) *the Justice principle* and (4) *the Relationship principle.*

The "Concern for Others" or Moral Law Principle
We primarily used this principle in the preceding paragraphs when we explored the lack of concern certain religious perspectives show towards others. Our application of this principle allowed us to reject a number of religious perspectives because they failed the standards of this principle. This principle recognizes that inner sense of duty toward others we all acknowledge. In earlier times, this might have been called the *moral law.* The idea that we are obligated to help others was an integral part of *morality.*[1]

What are some of the standards of this principle? They have been acknowledged in a number of different ways and settings. Some of these basic standards include:
- Do not murder.
- Do not steal.
- Do not lie or commit fraud.
- Honor and support your parents and family members.
- Treat the weak, the elderly, the infirm with care and respect.
- Love your neighbor as yourself.
- Love God.

We intuitively know that these standards are absolute. For instance, we know that it is wrong to murder, to steal or treat the weak in a cruel manner. We know that it is wrong to torture children. We acknowledge the divine authority of the command to love our neighbor as ourselves. We instinctively acknowledge our duty to love God. Based on this, we can infer that God (whoever he is) would agree that these standards are absolute. Further, since we know these standards are absolute we realize that their ultimate source of their truthfulness must lie in God.

Our exploration of the *"Concern for others" or Moral Law principle* also demonstrates that the Moral law is not something God created for the human race, they are standards he holds. In other words, we know that human sacrifice is wrong not simply because "God says so" but because God finds such acts repulsive.

These guidelines are taught among all of the world's celebrated religions – Judaism, Christianity, Islam, various branches of Buddhism and Hinduism – as well as many less known religions as well. Therefore, we know, at least at a certain level, these religions are teaching truths that are compatible with God's person. Jesus taught, *"Love the Lord your God with all your heart and with all your soul and with all your mind.' This is the first and greatest commandment. And the second is like it: 'Love your neighbor as yourself.' All the Law and the Prophets hang on these two commandments."* (*Matthew 22:39-40*)

At this point, however, certain other religious perspectives show that they are not one of the possible roads to God. For instance, religions which focus on self above others, which focus on the pursuit of pleasure above all else – are shown to be insufficient. No doubt, God wants us to enjoy life, but most people are aware of a sense of duty that rises higher than the enjoyment of life. So the *"Concern for others" or Moral Law principle* reminds us again that not all religions lead to God – namely religions which put the self before others.

The Self Awareness Principle
The Self Awareness principle demonstrates our intuitive sense that God must be an intelligent, self aware being. Our exploration of the *"Concern for Others" or Moral Law Principle* reveals God must have a definite mind and will. We have spoken of God as *knowing* about the importance of caring for others. We have indicated that we believe God is *offended* by those who would commit murder in his name. We acknowledge that God *cares* whether we love our neighbor and God himself. All of these verbs – *knowing*, *offended*, and *cares* – acknowledge that God possesses self awareness and mental activity. In other words, we intuitively know God is intelligent, has personality and a definite will.

This is in contrast to various religions, which teach God is an impersonal force that cannot be understood in terms of personality, awareness, good or evil. The parable of the elephant and the blind man is a story about man's search for God. The human race is represented by a number of blind men who hear there is an elephant (representative of God in this parable) on display in the town square. The blind men, who have never experienced an elephant before, decide to go and experience the elephant using the other senses available to them. Upon arrival one blind man discovers the elephant's trunk, another his legs, another his tail, and yet another his tusks. When they each compare notes, they all describe the elephant differently. The parable of the elephant concludes that our search for God is much the same – each person may experience an aspect of God differently, so who is to say when someone's perspective is incorrect?

Our interest in this parable lies in how God is pictured – as an unresponsive beast. This misunderstood elephant has no way to communicate with these men! The focus of this story falls on the human race and completely discounts the ability of God to communicate. Instead of comparing God to an animal, he should be compared to a person. A man or woman could communicate with these blind men and help them understand what he was really like. A person – with the ability of rational thought and communication – could have engaged the blind men in conversation and tell them what he was like!

This parable really has a very unflattering view of God, as he is assumed unable or unwilling to communicate. This parable is a favorite among Eastern and New Age religious perspectives as it reflects how they see God. While these religious views may embrace a strong moral outlook, they fail to describe God's person accurately.

The Christian message clearly passes the *Self Awareness principle*. The Lord said, "*I am the LORD; that is my name! I will not give my glory to another or my praise to idols.*" (*Isaiah 42:8*)

The Justice Principle
The Justice principle establishes the fact of our accountability to God for our failure to keep the Moral law. When confronted with the "*Concern for others*" or *Moral Law principle*, we are reminded

that we are responsible to live in a way that gives primary concern to other people and God. Our own consciences tell us we have failed to live up to these standards. Our failure to live up to these standards results in suffering for other people and God.

Since God is sentient (*the Self Awareness principle*), we infer that we are accountable to him for our violations of the Moral law. This brings us to awareness that we must face a judgment for our failure and sin – the *Justice principle*. The *Justice principle* reminds us of our accountability to God and our need for mercy. A religious perspective that is accurate must give helpful information on this critical issue. The Bible says, *"...man is destined to die once, and after that to face judgment."* (*Hebrews 9:27*)

The Relationship Principle
For a religious perspective to be viable, it must finally pass the *Relationship principle*. To this point, our discussion has revolved around the fact of the human race's involvement in relationships with each other and God. In fact, if we were to remove our relationships from the discussion, this conversation would collapse! The very existence of the Moral law assumes our relationships with others. Consequently, we find we are made for relationships. This reflects the words of the Bible, "*It is not good for the man to be alone.*" (*Genesis 2:18*)

This also gives us another clue about God. Earlier we discussed that the Moral law is a part of God's very character. If the Moral law is a reflection of God's personality, than he also must be a being of relationships. This is *the Relationship principle*. According to this principle, God must not only be a being capable of relationships, but must be a being in which relationships are fundamentally a part of his being.

The religious perspective of Islam pictures God as being one God, one being. Yet if this is true, than before the creation of the world, God must have been alone. Yet this is a contradiction to what our instincts tell us – for God must be a God of relationships. It is a contradiction for God to be alone.

The Christian message perfectly meets this principle. The Bible tells us God is *one God in three persons – Father, Son and Holy*

Spirit (see above, *Chapter three: Understanding Jesus Christ*). In other words, *God has forever existed in relationship*. When the Apostle John wrote, "*God is Love...*" (*1 John 4:16*), he was not speaking of God's potential to love but an eternal fact. This love has always been experienced by God in the community of mutual respect and love between Father, Son and Holy Spirit.

What you and I experience in our daily relationships is an extension of what God has always experienced in his very self. In other words, we are made in God's image.[2]

Conclusion – Do All Religions Lead to God?
We see that not all religions lead to God. At best, some religions teach the concept of a supreme being. Some aspects of various religions point away from God. Each person's religious views must pass the scrutiny of four principles:
- (1) *the "Concern for others" or Moral Law principle*;
- (2) *the Self Awareness principle;*
- (3) *the Justice principle* and;
- (4) *the Relationship principle*.

How does your belief system face the standards of these principles?

---

[1] My use of the *"Concern for Others" or the Moral law principle* may be objected to on the grounds everyone does not believe in the Moral law. In reply, it may be answered that because a person does not believe in something does not cause its existence to cease. If I meet someone who does not believe in Moral absolutes, I wonder (as do most people) what is wrong with him!

It also may be objected not everyone believes in the same moral law. While it is true different cultures may have slightly different standards, it is universally accepted that adultery, lying, murder, selfishness, etc. should be condemned. For a powerful discussion of this issue, please read, Lewis, C.S. *Mere Christianity*. Chapter One: The Law of Human Nature. I would also refer you to Lewis' work, *the Abolition of Man*, which addresses these issues in detail.

[2] See *Genesis 1:27*.

Chapter 5
The Universal Sense of Guilt

In our last chapter, we referred to *the Justice principle*. The *Justice principle* establishes that:
    (1) People are aware of the Moral law;
    (2) We are aware of having failed to fulfill the Moral law; and
    (3) We are aware that we will have to give an account of our failures to God.

Most people would agree that at points in their life they have violated an inner sense of Moral law. Perhaps you were cruel to someone, or you have stolen something, you lied or slandered someone unfairly – or any number of things. If you or I were to look even further, we might find that deep under our obvious failures also lies a troubling sense of deep selfishness. People often find there is a part of themselves that recognizes the Moral law but simply does not wish to obey it.

The Bible reflects what we intuitively know so well. Concerning our own internal sense of the Moral law, the Bible says, *"Even when Gentiles, who do not have God's written law, instinctively follow what the law says, they show that in their hearts they know right from wrong. They demonstrate that God's law is written within them, for their own consciences either accuse them or tell them they are doing what is right."* (Romans 2:14-15 – NLT)

The Bible also agrees with our assessment that while we know the Moral law part of us wants to obey it, while another part of ourselves does not. *"I don't understand myself at all, for I really want to do what is right, but I don't do it. Instead, I do the very thing I hate. I know perfectly well that what I am doing is wrong, and my bad conscience shows that I agree that the law is good."* (Romans 7:15-16 – NLT)

This leads us to the question of our impending judgment before God. We all know we are accountable. We wonder, however, what price must be paid for our failures and if we can pay it. I am reminded of a powerful example from the movie,

Unforgiven.[1] In this movie, Clint Eastwood plays the role of a retired gunslinger, William 'Bill' Munny. Munny has been hired to avenge the rape and savage beating of a woman. Joined by "the Schofield Kid" (Jaimz Woolvett), Munny finds and kills one of the men responsible for the crime. Clearly shaken by his part in this, "the Kid" exclaims, "I *guess he had it coming!*" Munny replies in a depressed fashion, "*We've all got it coming, Kid...*"
Eastwood's character hit upon a powerful truth – indeed, we've all got it coming.

World Religious Perspectives
Many religions attempt to deal with the Moral law, our failure to keep the Moral law and the issue of future accountability. One approach to these issues is seen in the Eastern religious concept of *Karma*. *Karma* is the belief in reward or punishment based on how well a person has kept the Moral law. According to this perspective, after death a person is reincarnated into another earthly life. The situation of your reincarnated life will be better or worse (in comparison to your current life) depending on how well you have kept the Moral law in this life.

Most religious perspectives offer a similar approach of reward or retribution based on how well a person has kept the Moral law. Most religions admit the existence of the Moral law and our failure to keep it. When it comes to the question of judgment, it is commonly expected that we will face God's judgment and give a full accounting of our life. If a person has failed to keep the Moral law in any way, the punishments predicted are usually severe – such as an eternal death in Hell, or an "endless" cycle of reincarnations. Some perspectives counter the severity of the situation by predicting God may have mercy on some persons. In many religious views, this mercy is contingent on the performing of certain rituals either by yourself before death or by someone else after you die. In other perspectives, it is contingent on the whim of God.

The Christian Message – the Only Alternative
Our review of the various religious perspectives leaves us with a sense of despair. Our own sense of righteousness tells us our failure to keep the Moral law has serious consequences. Yet we cannot escape the idea that we should be able to find mercy and forgiveness. We would also hope there is a way to escape from

Chapter Five: The Universal Sense of Guilt

our selfish patterns of living and thinking that are in opposition to the Moral law.

It is precisely at this point of crisis that the Christian message shows its relevance. "*Oh, what a miserable person I am! Who will free me from this life that is dominated by sin? Thank God! The answer is in Jesus Christ our Lord.*" (Romans 7:24-25 – NLV)

The Christian message preserves both the integrity of the Moral law and our heart's cry for mercy. The Bible tells us we have indeed failed to keep God's moral and spiritual commands. Further, we will have to give an account of our lives to God. The Bible tells us the result of our moral and spiritual failures – the Bible calls this "*sin*" – is separation from God and other people. After we die, those who reject God are separated from God and his people forever. Those who have accepted God's forgiveness and choose to live for him, join God and his people forever in Heaven.

To the modern mind, the idea of eternal separation from God is offensive. However, we should remember eternal punishment is assumed by most religious perspectives. Our own moral sense reminds us our failure of the Moral law has serious consequences. Therefore, we see the idea of penalty and punishment is not an invention of the Christian message – it is actually a fundamental conviction of the human race. What the Christian message offers, however, is truly unique. The Christian message offers the news of *God's grace*. Only through the Christian message is a way for forgiveness and restoration found.

How does God preserve the integrity between the Moral law and our need for mercy? The Bible tells us God did this through the life and work of Jesus. The Bible tells us Jesus died on the cross to pay the price you and I owe for our sin. Three days later, he bodily rose from the grave. Through turning from our sinful way of living and trusting in Jesus as the source of our forgiveness, we are put right with God from this day forward! "*For all have sinned; all fall short of God's glorious standard. Yet now God in his gracious kindness declares us not guilty. He has done this through Christ Jesus, who has freed us by taking away our sins. For God sent Jesus to take the punishment for our sins and to satisfy God's anger against us...For the wages of sin is death, but the free gift of God is eternal life through Christ Jesus our Lord." (Romans 3:23-25, 6:23 - NLT)*

Why did Jesus have to die – why didn't God just forgive our sins instead? I believe the answer lies in the fact that all of our moral and spiritual failures have a cost. This cost must be accepted by someone – either the party offended, or the person who commits the offense. For example, consider if a person broke into my home and wrecked my living room. In the process, let us assume this person destroys some items of both high dollar and sentimental value. While exiting my home, he is caught by the police.

The question becomes what I will choose to do. I may press charges as the law allows. This would entail the person paying a penalty for his crime (jail time or a fine) and replacing the items that he damaged.

I could also offer to forgive the person. Instead of pressing any charges, I could choose to bear the cost myself. I could replace out of my own pocket the items he destroyed. I could decide not to hold against him the sentimental (irreplaceable) items he destroyed. With this second option, I choose to bear the full cost. I pay the price financially and emotionally. This is what God, through Jesus, has done. Yes, God chooses to forgive us – but the price must still be paid. *"But God demonstrates his own love for us in this: While we were still sinners, Christ died for us." (Romans 5:8)*

Some expect God to overlook our sin. A person who expects this is really saying they expect favoritism from God. In other words, such a person wants God to turn a blind eye to justice just for them. Such an idea would have God ignore the times when you (or I) lied, stole, hated, coveted or did any number of like things that hurt God and humanity.

What I find interesting about this idea is that while we may want God to do this for ourselves, and maybe some family and friends, we don't want him to do this for the whole human race. If he did this, where would justice stand? Imagine all of the murderers, extortionists, rapists, dictators (and so on) who would be let off with no penalty.

Imagine the people who have hurt you and I so deeply being let off without a trace of accountability for their actions, with just a "nod and a wink!" We may want God to play favorites with us – but not with others. God will not do this, for God loves everyone. It turns out justice stems not from a lack of compassion, but from an abundance of it. Since God will not play favorites, he treats all equally. This is the exact position of the Christian view. In order to provide the forgiveness we all seek, God lovingly provided Jesus his Son[2] to pay the penalty we owe – so justice was perfectly satisfied, and we can be forgiven.

Accepting the Offer
The Bible tells us that it is not enough to know these facts. Each person is responsible to turn to God from living in opposition to his moral and spiritual laws and ask Jesus to forgive their sins.

It may be asked, *"Why won't God just universally apply Jesus' work on the cross to all people?"* We intuitively know this would not be appropriate. Imagine if the President of the United States granted a complete pardon to an unrepentant criminal! God is not interested in forgiving someone just so they can continue to make others miserable. Forgiveness is offered when we make a "good faith" pledge of repentance. We must all turn from our own way of doing things to God's way. *"Each of you must turn from your sins and turn to God..."* (Acts 2:3 - NLV)

Finding Harmony with God and People
The Bible promises the result of taking these truths seriously will be our finding harmony in our relationships with God and other persons. As to our relationship with God, the Bible says that when we accept Jesus' leadership and forgiveness, we are forgiven of all our wrongs, and made right in God's sight. The Bible says God actually makes those who choose Jesus his own children! *"Christ also suffered when he died for our sins once for all time. He never sinned, but he died for sinners that he might bring us safely home to God..."* (1 Peter 3:18 – NLV) *"But to all who believed Jesus and accepted him, he gave the right to become children of God."* (John 1:12 – NLV)

As to our relationships with others, isn't it self evident our relationships with others will improve when we live in the way God designed? Imagine how your relationships would improve if you simply decided to "*Love your neighbor as yourself.*" (*Matthew 22:39*) The Bible also says, "*Don't be selfish; don't live to make a good impression on others. Be humble, thinking of others as better than yourself. Don't think only about your own affairs, but be interested in others, too, and what they are doing.*" (*Philippians 2:3-4-NLV*)

---

[1] *Unforgiven*. Written by David Webb Peoples. Directed by Clint Eastwood. Warner Home Video. 1992.
[2] In presenting Jesus, God also presented himself. See the discussion above on the Trinity in *Chapter 3, Understanding Jesus Christ: Jesus the Son of God*. This is an important aspect of the Christian message to acknowledge. Otherwise, God appears to be cowardly – or worse.

In telling the story of God's mercy on the human race, the Bible emphasizes the distinctive nature of the persons of the Trinity. The Bible tells us God the Father serves as judge, Jesus the Son serves as mediator between God and the Christian, and the Holy Spirit serves as the equipper and strength giver to the Christian. These distinctions should not be overemphasized, however, as the Bible also refers to Father, Son and the Holy Spirit as serving in each of these capacities.

Chapter 6
The Debate about the Origins of the Universe

A frequent roadblock to faith is the perceived disagreement between the Christian and scientific communities about the origins of our universe. Contrary to this commonly held idea, there is a surprising amount of agreement between the Biblical perspective and the findings of modern science. This chapter is devoted to understanding the points at which both the Bible and modern science agree in their understanding of the origins of the human race and the universe around us.

Scientific Research and the Creation Perspective
The Anthropic Principle
One of the exciting aspects of living in our time is the growing scientific evidence for the "human friendly" design of our universe and world. This is called the *Anthropic principle*. This word "*Anthropic*" derives from the Greek word *anthropos*, which means "human being." Consider the following scientific facts:

- If the gravitational force of the universe were changed by 1 part in 10^{40} (a 10 followed by forty zeroes) the sun would not exist, and the moon would not be able to stay in orbit around the earth. If the gravitational force were increased even slightly, the result would be our sun (and all other stars) would burn much differently than they do. Our own sun could not support life on earth.[1]

- The placement of Jupiter in its orbital position has caused many to postulate Jupiter's orbit is the result of design, not chance. If Jupiter were not in the current orbit it is now in, the earth would be continually bombarded by material from space. Jupiter's gravitational field acts as a magnet or vacuum cleaner – attracting objects that would otherwise impact the earth.[2]

- The orbital distance between the Earth and the Sun is another astonishing example of design in the universe around us. If the Earth were slightly closer to the sun, all of the water on earth would boil away. If the Earth were slightly farther away, all of the water on earth would freeze.[3]

- Consider the abundant availability of water. Water is the only known substance in which its solid phase – ice – is less dense than its liquid phase. As a result, ice floats on the top of oceans and lakes, instead of on the bottom.[4] If ice sank instead of floated on water, the majority of the earth's water supply would remain frozen at the bottom of the world's oceans and lakes. Without water, humanity could not survive.

The Bible says, "*When I look at the night sky and see the work of your fingers – the moon and the stars you have set in place – what are mortals that you should think of us, mere humans that you should care for us? For you made us only a little lower than God, and you crowned us with glory and honor.*" (*Psalm 8:3-5*)

The Fossil Record and the Creation of Life
People suppose the idea of the evolution of species by gradual change is supported by the fossil record. One of the surprising facts of the fossil record is how it undermines this perspective. Harvard paleontologist (and proponent of evolutionary theory), Stephen Jay Gould has elaborated on the failure of the fossil record to support evolutionary theory. "*The extreme rarity of transitional forms in the fossil record persists as the trade secret of paleontology. The evolutionary trees that adorn our textbooks have data only at the tips and nodes of their branches; the rest is inference, however reasonable, not the evidence of fossils.*"[5] In other words, Gould admits the theory of evolution is not supported by the fossil record.

Again Stephen Jay Gould states, "*The history of most fossil species includes two features particularly inconsistent with gradualism:*

> *1. Stasis. Most species exhibit no directional change during their tenure on earth. They appear in the fossil record looking pretty much the same as when they disappear; morphological change is usually limited and directionless.*

> 2. Sudden appearance. In any local area, a species does not arise gradually by the steady transformation of its ancestors; it appears all at once and 'fully formed.'"[6]

The fossil record reveals life appeared on earth – out of "nowhere" – without any evidence of the transitional forms required by evolutionary theory. This is in accord with the Biblical record. The sudden appearance of fully formed and functional life within a compatible ecosystem strongly points to the creative work of an intelligent power.[7] Genesis 1:21, 24-25 states: "*So God created the great creatures of the sea and every living and moving thing with which the water teems, according to their kinds, and every winged bird according to its kind. And God saw that it was good...And God said, "Let the land produce living creatures according to their kinds: livestock, creatures that move along the ground, and wild animals, each according to its kind." And it was so. God made the wild animals according to their kinds, the livestock according to their kinds, and all the creatures that move along the ground according to their kinds. And God that saw it was good.*"

The Irreducible Complexity of Life
The Bible's proclamation of God's creation of the world is further supported by the field of biochemistry. In his 1996 book, *Darwin's Black Box – the Biochemical Challenge to Evolution*, biochemist Michael J. Behe argues that biological systems are irreducibly complex. Behe gives the example of a mousetrap. What is the purpose of a mousetrap? The purpose of a mousetrap is to catch mice. In order for a mousetrap to work, it requires a certain number of functioning parts. If any parts are missing, or do not function, the mousetrap will not work.

Behe's work shows how much of life – from "simple" cells to the human body – is irreducibly complex. Behe points to aspects of DNA reduplication, electron transport, telomere synthesis, photosynthesis, transcription regulation and the human eye. Behe states, "*No one at Harvard University, no one at the National Institutes of Health, no member of the National Academy of Sciences, no Nobel prize winner – no one at all can give a detailed account of how the cilium, or vision, or blood clotting, or any complex biochemical process might have developed in a Darwinian fashion. But we are here. Plants and* animals are here. The complex systems are here. All these things got here somehow, if not in a Darwinian fashion, then how?"[8]

All of life demonstrates irreducible complexity. Therefore, Behe concludes, evolution is shown to be an invalid theory for determining the origins of life. *"For you created my inmost being; you knit me together in my mother's womb. I praise you because I am fearfully and wonderfully made; your works are wonderful, I know that full well."* (Psalm 139:13-14)

Information Theory and DNA
There is also the challenge of information theory and DNA. Information theory is the *"...application of mathematical principles to the problems of transmitting and storing information."*[9] In information theory a structure or message is said to have high or low information content – determined by the minimum number of instructions needed to tell you how to understand it.

Charles Colson and Nancy Pearcey explain: *"...A random sequence of letters has low information content because it requires only two instructions: (1) select a letter of the English alphabet and write it down, and (2) do it again (select another letter and write it down). By the same token, a regular, repetitive patter of letters has low information content as well. Using your computer to create Christmas wrapping paper requires only a few instructions: (1) type in "M-e-r-r-y C-h-r-is-t-m-a-s," and (2) do it again. By contrast, if you want your computer to print out the poem "The Night before Christmas," you must specify every letter, one by one. Because the process of writing down the poem requires a large number of instructions, it is said to have high information content."*[10] High information content requires deliberate, intelligent input.

DNA has extremely high information content. One cell of the human body contains three to four times the information content of the full thirty volumes of the *Encyclopedia Britannica*.[11] Imagine your reaction if someone told you a set of the *Encyclopedia Britannica* or a copy of the *Complete Works of Shakespeare* in your library came about by random chance! To put it simply, DNA's information content is much too high to be

Chapter Six: The Debate about the Origins of the Universe

the result of random chance – it must be the work of an intelligent designer.

Comparing Genesis' Account of the Creation with Current Science

It is amazing how many of the claims of modern science line up with the account of creation God reveals in the book of Genesis. There is a high degree of corroboration between Genesis' account of the creation of the universe and current scientific understanding of the origins of the universe.

Did the Universe Have a Beginning?

Take for instance the claim of Genesis that the Universe had a beginning. This idea did not become a valid opinion in physics until the work of Albert Einstein in the early 20th Century.[12] Until this time it was believed the universe had always existed in the same state we see it now. Yet some three thousand, five hundred years before modern science's discovery, *Genesis 1:1* states: "*In the beginning God created the heavens and the earth.*"

The Initial Moments after the Big Bang

Another astonishing fact is the Genesis description states the occurrence of Light – completely apart from the sun and the stars – was a part of the initial moment of creation. Physicists have noted if you had been present at the instant of the big bang event, one characteristic you would have noticed was light in the darkness. *Genesis 1:3* states: "*And God said, 'Let there be light,' and there was light...*"

Water in Outer Space?

Genesis calls for the presence of water in the early stages of the universe's formation and implies its continued existence today throughout the cosmos. We know water is part of our ecosystem on earth, but skeptics often scoff at Genesis' account of water above the skies of the earth – i.e. outer space. *Genesis 1:6-8* says, "*And God said, "Let there be an expanse between the waters to separate water from water." So God made the expanse and separated the water under the expanse from the water above it. And it was so. God called the expanse "sky..."*"

This account of Genesis is now shown to be more accurate than previously believed. Researchers with the *European Space Agency's Infrared Space Observatory (ESAISO)* have discovered one of the natural working processes of stars is the production of water. *ESAISO's* researchers have also found there are large quantities of water to be found throughout the interstellar space in our galaxy – indeed, water was found to be the third most common molecule in the regions of the Milky Way galaxy studied.[13] Again, Genesis is shown to be astonishingly accurate in regard to its reporting of cosmological phenomena.

Life First Appeared in the Oceans
The Book of *Genesis* and modern scientific understanding calls for the first appearance of life in the oceans. *Genesis 1:20-21* states: "*And God said, 'Let the water teem with living creatures...So God created the great creatures of the sea and every living and moving thing with which the water teems, according to their kinds...'* "

The Fossil Record and the Creation of Life
As acknowledged above, the fossil records and the Bible agree in regard to the idea of life appearing on the earth, fully formed and with great complexity. In accordance with the account of Genesis, modern paleontologists have concluded all life – from cellular life to fully developed animals and humans – appeared on earth without any evidence for the evolution of such species over a long period.

All of Human Life Descended from Two Ancestors
Genesis also states all human life descends from two ancestors – Adam and Eve. Today, molecular biologists claim to have discovered one of the two members of this couple – namely, Eve. Using mitochondrial DNA – genetic material in a cell is passed on from mother to child unchanged – molecular biologists have traced the ancestors of all humans alive today to a common ancestor.[14] *Genesis 3:20* testifies, *Adam named his wife Eve, because she would become the mother of all the living.*"

The Human Race Originally Spoke One Language
Would you believe the human race originally spoke one language? The Book of *Genesis* says we did. Many modern linguists believe this was the case, citing numerous similarities

among languages and communication habits of people across the world.[15] *Genesis 11:1* states: "*Now the whole world had one language and a common speech.*"

A Common Picture of the Origins of the Universe
In closing this chapter, we return to the conversation between the Bible and science. It is often assumed there is hostility between the Biblical and scientific views of the origins of the universe. We now realize there is an amazing amount of compatibility between the Biblical record and modern scientific findings. While there may remain points of disagreement between scientific theory and the Bible, these points should not be overemphasized in one's quest for appreciating the truth of the Christian message.

---

[1] Geisler, Norman L.. *"Anthropic Principle."* Baker Encyclopedia of Christian Apologetics. Grand Rapids, Michigan: Baker Books, 1999. p. 26.
[2] Geisler, Norman L. *"Anthropic Principle."* Baker Encyclopedia of Christian Apologetics. p. 26.
[3] Colson, Charles and Pearcey, Nancy. *How Now Shall We Live?* Wheaton, Illinois: Tyndale House Publishers, Inc., 1999. p.62.
[4] Colson, Charles and Pearcey, Nancy. *How Now Shall We Live?* p.63.
[5] Geisler, Norman L... *"Evolution, Biological."* Baker Encyclopedia of Christian Apologetics. p. 226.
[6] Gould, Stephen Jay. As quoted by: Johnson, Phillip. *Darwin on Trial.* InterVarsity Press: Downers Grove, Illinois, 1993. p. 50.
[7] There are many books written on this lack of evidence for evolution. I would recommend Johnson, Phillip. *Darwin on Trial*
[8] Behe, Michael J. *Darwin's Black Box – the Biochemical Challenge to Evolution.* Touchstone Books: New York, New York, 1996. p. 187.
[9] *"Information Theory."* Microsoft Encarta Encyclopedia 2001. 1993-2000 Microsoft Corporation.
[10] Colson, Charles and Pearcey, Nancy. *How Now Shall We Live?* p.77.
[11] Colson, Charles and Pearcey, Nancy. *How Now Shall We Live?* p.75.
[12] *"Big Bang Theory."* Microsoft Encarta Encyclopedia 2001. 1993-2000 Microsoft Corporation.
[13] "*Europe's Space Telescope ISO Finds Water In Distant Places*" European Space Agency Plain Text Information Note. April 29, 1997. As found at: http://www.iso.vilspa.esa.es/outreach/esa_pr/in9712.htm. See also, "*Water in Space More Abundant than Expected.*" Space.com. April 12, 2001. As found at:

http://www.space.com/scienceastronomy/astronomy/milkyway_water_0 10412.html.

[14] "*Human Evolution.*" Microsoft Encarta Encyclopedia 2001. 1993-2000 Microsoft Corporation.

[15] Wade, Nicholas. "*What We All Spoke When the World Was Young.*" Science Section. The New York Times. February 1, 2000.

Chapter 7
Some Important Questions

Is it Possible for Miracles to Occur?
In the last chapters, the element of the miraculous has taken a major portion of our thought. We have spoken about the miracles Jesus performed on behalf of others and his own resurrection. By definition, these events testify to the belief God has worked in a way contrary to the normal passage of events in this world.

Some object that miracles cannot happen. It is believed the occurrence of such events would violate the laws of nature. Others believe that either God does not exist, or if he does, he does not interfere in the affairs of our universe. Beliefs like this may reflect personal opinion, but they cannot be said to determine facts.

The person who dogmatically says, "*Miracles cannot occur because they violate natural law*," is demonstrating ignorance of what miracles and natural law really are. Miracles are the action of a third party (God) in the normal course of events. The laws of nature dictate what occurs if events are left to their course – without interference. Natural law does not prohibit the actions of an intelligent, empowered third party.

For example, it is well known that meat rots when left unprotected or un-refrigerated. This occurs by the working of natural processes that result in the decay of the meat. Yet no one claims natural law has been violated if no decay occurs when I place the meat in a freezer. In the same way, no one complains that natural law is violated when a doctor interferes with the natural process of a patient's illness. Doctors regularly interfere with natural law when they administer antibiotics, engage in helpful surgical procedures or otherwise work to heal a patient.[1]

The same can be said of miracles. A miracle occurs when God intervenes in a situation to help people in need. In this case, God is the third party and he works to supply, add to, or otherwise change an existing situation. After the miracle has occurred, the person or situation is once again subject to the normal course of events.

The person who states, "*God does not exist*" or "*if God exists he does not work miracles*" is in a position of absurd contradiction. To say that *God does not exist* is to claim to know something one cannot possibly know. To know that God does not exist would require a complete knowledge of everything in the universe (and beyond).[2] The most any person can claim about the existence of God is that God's existence has not been proven to him.

The claim *if God exists he does not work miracles* is also to claim something one cannot know. Notice that this is a claim of personal knowledge – i.e., *I know what God does and does not do*. To be able to make such a statement one would have to make one or two specific claims – (1) to have a total knowledge of all that exists or (2) to have spoken with God. We dealt with the first claim in the paragraph above. The second claim, to have spoken with God, would be to claim to have experienced a miracle. Such an event would invalidate the very claim they were making!

In short, people who disbelieve that God works miracles can only claim their perspective as an *opinion*. It is rationally impossible to state their claims as *fact*. Therefore, we see that miracles are indeed possible and there is no intelligent reason why we should not be open minded to their existence.

The Bible's Record of Miracles
What does the Bible have to say about miracles? The Bible clearly claims that God works miracles and that these miracles are a matter of historical record. However, the Bible does not discard natural law or endorse accepting the claim of a miracle uncritically.

The Bible affirms natural law. The Bible assumes an orderly structure to the universe around us. The Bible tells us that Jesus was born of a virgin woman. An interesting aspect of this story is how Mary's fiancé, Joseph, reacted to this news. He planned to break off the engagement (*Matthew 1:18-25*)![3] Joseph had no illusions about "where babies come from." It was only after an angel explained the situation to Joseph that he decided to continue with the marriage. Natural law provides a backdrop for the occurrence of miracles. The Bible celebrates God's creation of the universe with fixed laws of operation.

The Bible encourages a cautious approach to miracles. The Bible acknowledges we have to investigate claims of miracles and not simply accept such claims at face value. When it is claimed a miracle has happened, the Bible calls for determining whether the event really was miraculous. In the event a miracle did occur, we are to determine whether it is a miracle accomplished by God or another source. The following Bible verses explain some of the practices commanded by the Bible as to how to handle claims of miraculous events.

"If what a prophet proclaims in the name of the LORD does not take place or come true, that is a message the LORD has not spoken. That prophet has spoken presumptuously. Do not be afraid of him." (Deuteronomy 18:22)

"If a prophet, or one who foretells by dreams, appears among you and announces to you a miraculous sign or wonder, and if the sign or wonder of which he has spoken takes place, and he says, "Let us follow other gods" (gods you have not known) "and let us worship them," you must not listen to the words of that prophet or dreamer. The LORD your God is testing you to find out whether you love him with all your heart and with all your soul. It is the LORD your God you must follow, and him you must revere. Keep his commands and obey him; serve him and hold fast to him." (Deuteronomy 13:1-4)

It is interesting to note that Jesus' opponents did not deny his miraculous powers but rather questioned the source of his power. They accused him of being in league with the devil. Jesus replied he could not be in league with the devil because he was undoing the devil's work! (see *Mark 3:22-27*)

How Can I Know God Exists?
In considering this question, I would point to three lines of evidence I believe to be beyond debate. The first line of evidence is Jesus' resurrection. As we discovered in *Chapter Two: Did Jesus Defeat Death?*, the Christian belief in Jesus' resurrection is based not upon feeling, but on the best

interpretation of the facts. Apart from God, how can we account for Jesus' resurrection?

The second line of evidence for God's existence is the design of ourselves, our world, and the cosmos around us. As we explored in *Chapter Six: The Debate about the Origins of the Universe*, both the detailed design and "human friendly" aspects of all that is around us point to an Intelligent Designer. We explored how the intricate nature of DNA and various forms of life all contain more information in their structure than can be accounted for by random chance. We know God exists, because if he did not, than we would not exist either!

The last line of evidence is the human race's clear sense of a Moral law and our accountability for it. This issue was explored in *Chapter Four: Don't All Religions Lead to God* and *Chapter Five: The Universal Sense of Guilt*. A Moral law demands a lawgiver. This lawgiver can be none other than God himself. Further, our own intuitive sense of Moral law lends to a picture of God remarkably like the God presented in the pages of the Bible. The Moral law clearly points to the existence of God.

The evidence for God's existence is exceptionally convincing. The evidence is so overwhelming that, when encountering a person who claims not to believe in God, it leads me to ask what bias keeps them from believing in God. In my experience, a person's lack of belief does not stem from a lack of evidence but from a bias against belief. If you don't believe in God, you might consider what motives you have for your disbelief!

Bible Prophecy – Did the Old Testament Accurately Predict Jesus' Coming?
The Old Testament foretold the coming of Jesus hundreds of years before he came. These predictions take the form of allusions, prefigurement and direct prophecies about Jesus. I once commented by the time the Old Testament is completed you get a rich and full picture of Jesus – before he arrives! Than Jesus comes and fulfills all the prophecies given about him. One writer estimates there are almost three hundred prophecies about Jesus in the Old Testament.[4]

Chapter Seven: Some Important Questions

Abraham's Test (Genesis 22:1-19)
The Bible tells of how God once commanded Abraham, an ancient ancestor of Jesus, to offer his son as a burnt offering. Now, this term "burnt offering" refers to the slaughtering of an animal and burning its remains as a sacrifice as an act of worship to God. This sacrifice was offered to pay the penalty of the sins of the person offering the animal. In this case, Abraham was told not to offer an animal, but his own son!

At this point, I must make clear, that the Bible says God hates human sacrifice.

> *"Do not give any of your children to be sacrificed to Molech, for you must not profane the name of your God. I am the LORD..."Say to the Israelites: 'Any Israelite or any alien living in Israel who gives any of his children to Molech must be put to death. The people of the community are to stone him."* (Leviticus 18:21, 20:2)

> *"They built high places for Baal in the Valley of Ben Hinnom to sacrifice their sons and daughters to Molech, though I never commanded, nor did it enter my mind, that they should do such a detestable thing and so make Judah sin."* (Jeremiah 32:35)

> *"They sacrificed their sons and daughters in the fire. They practiced divination and sorcery and sold themselves to do evil in the eyes of the LORD, provoking him to anger."* (2 Kings 17:17)

> *"For when you offer gifts to them and give your little children to be burned as sacrifices, you continue to pollute yourselves to this day. Should I listen to you or help you, O people of Israel?"* (Ezekiel 20:31-NLV)

Therefore, the story of Abraham and Isaac should not be taken to suggest God approves of human sacrifice.

Abraham knew God hated human sacrifice. As a result, he was posed with a dilemma when God told him to sacrifice his son. God was contradicting himself! How could he resolve this issue? It appears Abraham concluded this was a test – he did not believe God was interested in the sacrifice of his son. Clearly,

God was making some other point. On the way to offer his son as a sacrifice, Abraham spoke to those traveling with him and his son, Isaac. "*Stay here with the donkey while I and the boy go over there.* **We will worship and then we will come back to you**..." *Isaac said, "Where is the lamb for the burnt offering?" Abraham answered,* "**God himself will provide the lamb for the burnt offering, my son**..." (*Genesis 22:5, 7* – **bold emphasis, mine**)

The story tells us that Abraham went through the motions of sacrificing his son. Just before Abraham swung the knife at his son, God stopped him. The Lord told him that he was pleased that Abraham was willing to obey him. At this point, Abraham sees nearby a ram caught by its horns in a bush. Abraham then offers the ram instead of his son.

I cannot tell you all the reasons Abraham and Isaac went through such an ordeal. I can tell you, however, this story clearly points to Jesus. The Bible tells us that two thousand years later, Jesus did indeed come and literally fulfilled the meaning of this dramatic interchange between Abraham, Isaac and God.

The prominent figures in this story help us to understand the significance of Jesus.

Isaac foreshadows Jesus. Like Isaac who obeyed his Father, Jesus came because God his Father sent him. *Jesus said, "...the world must learn that I love the Father and that I do exactly what my Father has commanded me..."* (*John 14:31*)

Isaac also foreshadows Jesus in that he carried the wood upon which he was sacrificed (*Genesis 22:6*). The gospel accounts tell us that Jesus carried his cross - made of wood - to the place where he was crucified. "*Carrying his own cross, he went out to the place of the Skull (which in Aramaic is called Golgotha). Here they crucified him...*" (*John 19:17-18*)

In being willing to give his only son (*Genesis 22:12*), Abraham foreshadows God's action in sending his only Son. God gave his Son for the sins of the world. "*For God so loved the world that he gave his one and only Son, that whoever believes in him shall not perish but have eternal life. For God did not send his Son* into the world to condemn the world, but to save the world through him." (*John 3:16-17*)

The ram also foreshadows the role of Jesus in giving his life for ours. Like the ram in the story, Jesus gave his life as a substitute for our lives. Through his death and resurrection, we live! *"For you know that God paid a ransom to save you from the empty life you inherited from your ancestors. And the ransom he paid was not mere gold or silver. He paid for you with the precious lifeblood of Christ, the sinless, spotless Lamb of God."* (*1 Peter 1:18-19 - NLV*)

Over two thousand years before he came, this remarkable story points us to Jesus, the Son of God, who gave his life for our lives.

Jesus' Crucifixion (Psalm 22:1-31)
Written a thousand years before Jesus' death, this psalm dramatically portrays his crucifixion. Jesus himself pointed to this prophecy as he hung on the cross and called out the first verse: "*My God, my God, why have you forsaken me?*" (*Psalm 22:1, Matthew 27:45*)

This psalm is remarkable as it describes the events of Jesus crucifixion centuries before the practice was invented. The Psalm predicts:
- Jesus' public humiliation during his crucifixion (*Psalm 22:7-8, Matthew 27:41-44, Luke 23:35*);
- the strain on his body produced by the contortions of crucifixion (*Psalm 22:14a, 17*);
- the rupture of his heart due to the trauma of crucifixion (*Psalm 22:14b, John 19:34*);
- the piercing of Jesus' hands and feet as he was nailed to the cross (*Psalm 22:16b; John 19:23, 20:25, 20:27*);
- Jesus' victorious resurrection (*Psalm 22:24-25, Luke 24:46*);
- the Christian message and the hope it would bring to people throughout the world (*Psalm 22:27, Luke 24:47, Acts 1:8*).

Jesus Character and Crucifixion (Isaiah 53:1-12)
Seven hundred years before Jesus' birth, the Lord inspired the prophet Isaiah who gave many prophecies about Jesus. One of

these prophecies is found in *Isaiah 53*. This prophecy details some of the aspects of Jesus' humble beginnings, the manner of his death and his resurrection. *Isaiah 53* predicts these details about Jesus' life:
- the rejection Jesus would face from many of his contemporaries (*Isaiah 53:3; Luke 11:15; John 1:46, 6:60, 66; 7:52*);
- his humble background (his parents were of common background) (*Isaiah 53:2, Luke 4:22, John 6:42*);
- the collaboration of political forces that would deliver him to death – even though he was guilty of no crime (*Isaiah 53:7-8a, 9, John 18:1-19:16*);
- the effect of Jesus' death – to deliver us from the penalty of our sins, and their dominating influence in our lives (*Isaiah 53:4-6, 8b, 12; Romans 3:21-25, 6:1-14; 2 Corinthians 5:21*);
- his death among criminals (*Isaiah 53:9, Luke 23:32-43*);
- his burial in a rich man's tomb (*Isaiah 53:9, Matthew 27:57-61, John 19:38-42*);
- his resurrection (*Isaiah 53:11-12, Mark 16:6-7, John 20:19-22*);
- the offering of forgiveness through Jesus that would come after his resurrection (*Isaiah 53:11b, Luke 24:45-47*).

These are just three of the hundreds of passages that prophesied Jesus' coming. There are many other prophecies about Jesus in the Old Testament. These prophecies speak to the manner of his birth, the places he would live, the miracles he accomplished and other details of his life. To explore this subject further, see Josh McDowell's *The New Evidence that Demands a Verdict*. Chapter 8: Old Testament Prophecies Fulfilled in Jesus Christ. (Nashville, Tennessee: Thomas Nelson Publishers). 1999. p. 69-90.

---

[1] It may be countered that both examples – of the freezer and the doctor – work within the bounds of natural law. My focus, however, is on the fact of third party interference not being a contradiction to natural law.
[2] To claim total knowledge is to claim *omniscience*. According to the Bible, *omniscience* is one of the characteristics of God. So to state that God does not exist, is to claim to be omniscient. Ironically, the person who claims that God does not exist is in fact claiming to be God.

[3] Technically, the Bible says that Joseph was going to divorce Mary. The term "divorce" is used because in the latter stages of Jewish courtship, the couple was considered virtually married.
[4] McDowell, Josh D. *The New Evidence that Demands a Verdict*. Nashville, Tennessee: Thomas Nelson Publishers, 1999. p. 164.

Chapter 8
In the Final Analysis

The evidence for Jesus Christ is clear and compelling. Jesus' call to turn from our sins and trust him for forgiveness is as clear today as it was when he first proclaimed this message. The question now becomes what you will do with his message.

Do you want to learn more about Jesus? There are many resources available to further your understanding of the Christian message and to grow in the Christian life.

I Have More Questions
Do you still have intellectual reservations about the Christian message? Consider these resources:
- *The Case for Christ*, by Lee Strobel. (Grand Rapids, Michigan: Zondervan Publishing House. 1998).

- *The Case for Faith*, by Lee Strobel. (Grand Rapids, Michigan: Zondervan Publishing House. 2000).

- *Mere Christianity*, by C.S. Lewis. (San Francisco, California: HarperCollins Publishers. 1980).

- *The New Evidence that Demands a Verdict*, by Josh McDowell. (Nashville, Tennessee: Thomas Nelson Publishers). This book provides a detailed critique of various challenges to the Christian message.

Understanding the Christian Message
Do you want to learn more about the Christian message? Consider these resources:
- *Mere Christianity*, by C.S. Lewis. (San Francisco, California: HarperCollins Publishers. 1980).

- *Peace with God*, by Billy Graham. (Nashville, Tennessee; Word Publishing. 1984).

- *The Bible*. Find a Bible written in a style you are comfortable reading.[1] Start by reading the gospels of

Matthew, Mark, Luke and *John*. In addition, I recommend reading *Acts, 1 Peter* and *1 John*.
- *Go to Your Local Church*. Find a group of Christians who meet on a regular basis to study the Bible. Join them on a regular basis. Let them know of your desire to learn more about the Christian message.

---

[1] There are many acceptable modern translations. Three versions I enjoy are the *New International Version* (NIV) (Grand Rapids, Michigan; International Bible Society. 1984); *Today's New International Version* – a revision of the NIV (Grand Rapids, Michigan; International Bible Society. 2001); and the *New Living Translation* (NLT) (Wheaton, Illinois; Tyndale House Publishers, Inc. 1996). I have quoted from the NIV and NLT in this book.

Works Referenced or Recommended

Barclay, William. *The Revelation of John, volume 1.* The Daily Study Bible Series. Philadelphia, Pennsylvania: Westminster Press. 1976.

Bruce, F.F. *The Books and the Parchments: How We Got Our English Bible.* Old Tappan, New Jersey: Fleming H. Revell Co. 1950.

Bruce, F.F. *The New Testament Documents: Are They Reliable?* Downers Grove, Illinois: InterVarsity Press. 1981.

Beasley-Murray, John George R. *"II. The Public Ministry of Jesus, Sub Section C. Jesus the Mediator of Life and Judgment (4:43–5:47) Notes – note: g."* Gospel of John, Volume 36, Word Biblical Commentary. Dallas, Texas: Word Books, Publisher, 1987.

Behe, Michael J. *Darwin's Black Box – the Biochemical Challenge to Evolution.* Touchstone Books: New York, New York, 1996.

Butler, Trent C., editor. *Holman Bible Dictionary.* Nashville, Tennessee: Holman Bible Publishers, 1991.

Colson, Charles and Pearcey, Nancy. *How Now Shall We Live?* Wheaton, Illinois: Tyndale House Publishers, Inc., 1999.

Craig, William Lane and Ludeman, Gerd. Copan, Paul and Tacelli, Ronald K. editors. *Jesus' Resurrection – Fact or Figment?* Downers Grove, Illinois: InterVarsity Press, 2000.

Davidson, Samuel. The *Hebrew Text of the Old Testament.* London: 1856.

Dockery, David. *Foundations for Biblical Interpetation.* Nashville, Tennessee: Broadman and Holman Publishers, 1994.

Edwards, William D., Gabel, Wesley J., Hosmer, Floyd E. *On The Physical Death Of Jesus Christ.* Journal of the American Medical Association. Vol. 255 No. 11, pp. 1397-1488, March 21, 1986.

Elder, John. *Prophets, Idols and Diggers.* New York: Bobbs Merril Co. 1960.

"Europe's Space Telescope ISO Finds Water In Distant Places" European Space Agency Plain Text Information Note. April 29, 1997. As found at: http://www.iso.vilspa.esa.es/outreach/esa_pr/in9712.htm.

Works Referenced or Recommended

Fernando, Ajith. *The NIV Application Commentary.* Grand Rapids, Michigan: Zondervan Publishing House.

Geisler, Norman L.. *Baker Encyclopedia of Christian Apologetics.* Grand Rapids, Michigan: Baker Books, 1999.

Graham, Billy. *Peace with God.* (Nashville, Tennessee; Word Publishing. 1984).

Habermas, Gary R. and J.P. Moreland. *Beyond Death: Exploring the Evidence for Immortality.* Wheaton, Illinois: Crossway Books, 1998.

Johnson, Phillip. *Darwin on Trial.* InterVarsity Press: Downers Grove, Illinois, 1993.

Kitchen, K.A. *The Ancient Orient and the Old Testament.* Chicago, Illinois: InterVarsity Press. 1966.

Kitchen, K.A. *The Bible in its World.* Downers Grove, Illinois: InterVarsity Press, 1978.

Kreeft, Peter and Tacelli, Ronald K. *Handbook of Christian Apologetics.* Downers Grove, Illinois: InterVarsity Press, 1991.

Lewis, C.S. *The Abolition of Man.* San Francisco, California: HarperCollins Publishers. 1974.

Lewis, C.S. *Mere Christianity.* San Francisco, California: HarperCollins Publishers. 1980.

McDowell, Josh D. *The New Evidence that Demands a Verdict.* Nashville, Tennessee: Thomas Nelson Publishers, 1999.

Microsoft Encarta Encyclopedia 2001. 1993-2000 Microsoft Corporation.

Miller, Robert J., editor. *The Complete Gospels – Annotated Scholars Version.* San Francisco, California: HarperCollins, 1994.

Morissette, Alanis. *What If God Was One Of Us?* As found at: http://www.azlyrics.us/09804.

Elwell, Walter A. *Evangelical Dictionary of Theology.* Grand Rapids, Michigan: Baker Books, 1984.

Pritchard, James B. ed. *The Ancient Near East, vol. 2. A New Anthoogy of Texts and Pictures.*

Strobel, Lee. *The Case for Christ.* Grand Rapids, Michigan: Zondervan Publishing House. 1998.

Unforgiven. Written by David Webb Peoples. Directed by Clint Eastwood. Warner Home Video. 1992.

Wade, Nicholas. "*What We All Spoke When the World Was Young.*" Science Section. The New York Times. February 1, 2000.

Watts, John D.W. *Scene 4: A Reading (continued): Isaiah's Response from Yahweh (37:21-38) Comment – v. 38.* Isaiah 34–66, Volume 25, Word Biblical Commentary, Dallas, Texas: Word Books, Publisher, 1987. .

"*Water in Space More Abundant than Expected.*" Space.com. April 12, 2001. As found at: http://www.space.com/scienceastronomy/astronomy/milkyway_water_010412.html.

Wilson, Robert Dick. A Scientific Investigation of the Old Testament. Chicago, Illinois: Moody Press. 1959.

Wood, Bryant G. "*Did the Israelites Conquer Jericho?*" Biblical Archaeology Review. March / April 1990.

About Chris Schansberg
Chris has been the Pastor of Dauphin Island Baptist Church, Dauphin Island, Alabama since 1998. The church's web site is www.dibaptist.org.

Chris and his wife, Lee, have been in Christian ministry for ten years. Both Lee and Chris love being married to each other. Together, they are committed to serving the Lord Jesus Christ.

Alertness Books Quick Order Form

Ordering Options:
  Fax: 413-622-9441
  Phone: 866-492-2137 (toll-free) or 864-444-3728
  On-line: http://www.policyofliberty.net
  Postal: Alertness Books, Box 25686, Greenville, SC 29616

Please send me: **Quantity**

Books by Chris Schansberg
Reasons to Believe: Evidence for the Christian Faith — Paperback $9.95 ___

Books by Dr. Eric Schansberg
Turn Neither to the Right nor to the Left: A Thinking Christian's Guide to Politics & Public Policy — Paperback $15.00 ___
Turn Neither to the Right nor to the Left: A Thinking Christian's Guide to Politics & Public Policy — PDF $5.00 ___
Inheriting Our Promised Land: Lessons in Victorious Christian Life from the Book of Joshua — Paperback $10.00 ___
Inheriting Our Promised Land: Lessons in Victorious Christian Life from the Book of Joshua — PDF $5.00 ___

Books by Dr. John Cobin
Bible and Government: Public Policy from a Christian Perspective Paperback — Paperback $10.95 ___
Bible and Government: Public Policy from a Christian Perspective Paperback — PDF $3.95 ___
Pro life Policy A Perspective for Liberty and Human Rights — PDF $2.95 ___
Building Regulation Market Alternatives and Allodial Policy — PDF $3.95 ___

Name: _____
Address: _____
City/State/Zip: _____
Phone/Email: _____

Please add 5% for products shipped to South Carolina addresses.
Shipping by ground: $2 per book (with credit card); $2 for first book; $1 for each additional book (with check).
Quantity Discount: 20% on orders of 10 or more books.
Make checks payable to Alertness Ltd.

Credit Card: Visa / MasterCard / Optima / Amex / Discover (circle one)

Card Number: _____ Expiration Date: _____
Name on Card: _____

Ask for *Reasons to Believe: Evidence for the Christian Message*
at your local or online bookstore.

Distributed by Lightning Source

(USA)
Lightning Source Inc.
1246 Heil Quaker Blvd.
La Vergne, TN USA 37086
Voice: (615) 213-5815
Fax: (615) 213-4426
Email:
inquiry@lightningsource.com
https://www.lightningsource.com

(UK)
Lightning Source UK Ltd.
6 Precedent Drive
Rooksley
Milton Keynes
MK13 8PR, UK
Email:
enquiries@lightningsource.co.uk
Voice: +44 (0) 1908 443555
Fax: +44 (0) 1908 443594

Printed in the United States
17860LVS00001B/34-102